MARTIN HEIDEGGER

martin heidegger

george steiner

With a new Introduction

THE UNIVERSITY OF CHICAGO PRESS

FOR DAVID, WHO ASKED

Martin Heidegger was first published by The Viking Press in
the Modern Masters series, edited by Frank Kermode.

The Introduction, "Heidegger: In 1991," was first published
under the title "Heidegger, Again" in the Spring/Summer
1989 issue of *Salmagundi*.

THE UNIVERSITY OF CHICAGO PRESS, CHICAGO 60637

University of Chicago Press edition 1987
Printed in the United States of America
96 95 94 93 92 91   5 4 3

LIBRARY OF CONGRESS CATALOGING IN PUBLICATION DATA

Steiner, George, 1929–
    Martin Heidegger : with a new introduction /
George Steiner.
        p.   cm.
    Includes bibliographical references and index.
    1. Heidegger, Martin, 1889–1976. I. Title.
[B3279.H49S693 1991]
193—dc20   91-15638
                                       CIP
ISBN 0-226-77232-2 (pbk.)

CONTENTS

Heidegger: In 1991

I

The crisis of spirit suffered by Germany in 1918 was more profound than that of 1945. The material destruction, the revelations of inhumanity which accompanied the collapse of the Third Reich numbed the German imagination. Immediate necessities for bare survival absorbed what the war had left of intellectual and psychological resources. The condition of a leprous, divided Germany was too new, the Hitlerian atrocity was too singular, to allow of any coherent philosophic critique or revaluation. The situation in 1918 was catastrophic, but in a way which not only preserved the stability of the physical, historical setting (Germany was materially almost intact), but also pressed upon reflection and sensibility the facts of self-destruction and of continuity in European culture. The survivance of the national framework, of the academic and literary conventions, made feasible a metaphysical-poetic discourse on chaos. (None comparable followed on 1945.)

Of this discourse sprang a constellation of books unlike any others produced in the history of Western thought and feeling: Between 1918 and 1927, within nine short years, there appear in German half a dozen books that are more than books in their dimensions and manner of extremity. The first edition of Ernst Bloch's *Geist der Utopie* is dated 1918. So is volume one of Oswald Spengler's *Decline of the West*. The initial version of Karl Barth's Commentary on *Romans,* of Barth's reading of St. Paul, is dated 1919. Franz Rosenzweig's *Stern der Erlösung* follows in 1921. Martin Heidegger's *Sein und Zeit* is published in 1927. The question of whether the sixth title forms part of this configuration, and, if so, in what ways, is among the most difficult. *Mein Kampf* appears in its two volumes between 1925 and 1927.

Roughly perceived, what have these works in common? They are voluminous. This is no accident. It tells of an imperative endeavor toward totality (after Hegel), of an attempt to provide, even where the point of departure is of a specialized historical or philosophic order, a *summa* of all available insight. It was as if the urgent prolixity of these writers sought to build a capacious house of words where that of German cultural and imperial hegemony had collapsed. These are prophetic texts, at once utopian — the utopia of promise is as manifest in Bloch as is that of twilight, of a *nunc dimittis* from the burdens of history in Spengler — and, as is all authentic prophecy, retrospective, commemorative of a lost ideal. The climate of 1918 is such as to compel and permit a more or less enhanced remembrance of the civilities, of the cultural stabilities, of the pre-1914 world. (The abyss of 1933–45 cut off such remembrance.)

These works are, in a sense which is also technical, apocalyptic. They address themselves to "the last things."

Again, the apocalyptic prevision can be salutary, as in Rosenzweig's movement toward redemption or Ernst Bloch's blueprint for secular, though nevertheless messianic, emancipation; or it can be a figuration of catastrophe. In this respect, Barth's teaching of the utter incommensurability between God and man, between the infinity of the divine and the unalterable constraints of human perception, is darkly ambiguous. It tells of the necessity of hopes which are, in essence, illusory. We know of the dread foresight, of the contract with apocalypse in *Mein Kampf*. Like their leviathan counterpart in Austria, Karl Kraus's *The Last Days of Humanity*, these writings out of the German ruin are, indeed, meant to be read either by men and women doomed to decay, as in Spengler, or by men and women destined to undergo some fundamental renovation, some agonizing rebirth out of the ash of a dead past. This is Bloch's message, Rosenzweig's, and, in a perspective of eternal untimeliness, that of Barth. It is Hitler's promise to the *Volk*.

Massive scale, a prophetic tenor, and the invocation of the apocalyptic make for a specific violence. These are violent books. There is no more violent dictum in theological literature than Karl Barth's: "God speaks His eternal No to the world." In Rosenzweig, the violence is one of exaltation. The light of God's immediacy breaks almost unbearably upon human consciousness. Ernst Bloch sings and preaches revolution, the overthrow of the existing order within man's psyche and society. The *Spirit of Utopia* will lead directly to Bloch's fiery celebration of Thomas Münzer and the sixteenth-century insurrections of peasant-saints and millenarians. The baroque violence, the rhetorical satisfaction in disaster — literally "the falling of the stars" — in Spengler's *magnum* have often been noted. And there is no need to detail the raucous inhumanity in the eloquence of Herr Hitler.

This violence is, inevitably, stylistic. Though intensely

pertinent, the criteria of Expressionism are too broad. These *are* writings which interact decisively with the aesthetics, with the rhetoric of Expressionist literature, art, and music. Certain premonitory voices, those of Jakob Böhme, of Kierkegaard, and of Nietzsche, sound throughout Expressionism as they do in these six books. The ambience of apocalyptic extremity is pervasive. But that which I am trying to identify in Barth or Heidegger or Bloch is of a particular kind. It would be rewarding to probe closely the uses of negation in the thought and grammar of the Commentary on *Romans*, of Rosenzweig's analysis of mundanity, or of the strategies of annulment, of exorcism through annihilation in *My Struggle*. Here is no Hegelian negation, with its dialectical yield of positivity. The terms now so cardinal to our study of Heidegger — "nothing," "nothingness," *nichten*, untranslatable as the verb "to nothing" — have their analogue throughout the set. Barth's God is "the Judge of the *Nichtsein* [the non-being, the being-nothing] of the world." It is out of the "not-thereness" of the divine in classical and rational ontologies that Rosenzweig derives his program for salvation. No less lyrically than James Joyce's Molly Bloom, Ernst Bloch strives to enforce an overwhelming, life-saving Yes as against the *Nichtigkeit*, the "nothingness" and the denial (*Verneinen*) spoken upon history and human hopes by the madness of world war.

Both the sounding of nothingness, which has its history in metaphysical and in mystical speculations — Heidegger's work has its source in Leibniz's famous question: "why is there not nothing?" — and the summons to renascence have crucial linguistic applications. The language itself must be made new. It must be purged of the obstinate remnants of a ruined past. We know the extent to which this *kathartic* imperative is inherent in all modernism after Mallarmé. We know that there is scarcely a modern aesthetic manifesto or school, be it Symbolism, Futurism, Surrealism, which does not declare the renovation of poetic discourse to be among its principal purposes. In a vein at once precious and incisive, Hofmannsthal asks how it is *possible* to use the old, worn, mendacious words after the facts of 1914–18 (Wittgenstein listens closely to that question). But in the works I have cited, the attempts to make language new have a singular radicality. Where Spengler is still, and perhaps parodistically, a mandarin, a private academic whose erudite solemnities of voice play deliberately against the wildness of his *pronouncements* — a play often modeled on Goethe's *Faust* — writers such as Bloch and Rosenzweig are neologists, subverters of traditional grammar. In subsequent editions, Barth attenuates the lapidary strangeness of his idiom, an idiom meant very concretely to exemplify the abyss between human logic and the true God who is "the origin, abstaining from all objectivity [or "facticity"] of the crisis of all objectivity" ("*der aller Gegenständlichkeit entbehrende Ursprung der Krisis aller Gegenständlichkeit*"). Much in Hitler's language, in that anti-matter to the *Logos*, still needs to be analyzed. In short: more consciously, more violently than any other language, and in ways that may indeed have been influenced by Dada and its desperate call for a totally new human tongue with which to voice the desperation and hopes of the age, the German language after the first world war seeks a break with its past. Endowed with a peculiarly mobile syntax and with the capacity to fragment or to fuse words and word-roots almost at will, German looks to elect solitaries in its past, to Master Eckhardt, to Böhme, to Hölderlin, and to such innovations as Surrealism and the cinema in its present, for instigations to renewal. The *Stern der Erlösung*, Bloch's messianic tracts, Barth's exegetics, and, above all, *Sein und Zeit* are speech-acts of the most revolutionary kind.

It is only in this linguistic and emotive context that Heidegger's method becomes intelligible. *Sein und Zeit* is an immensely original product. But it has distinct affinities to the exactly contemporaneous constellation of the apocalyptic. Like them, it would overcome the language of the immediate German past and forge a new speech both by virtue of radical invention and by a selective return to "forgotten" sources. Karl Löwith was probably the first to remark on the similitudes in rhetoric and ontological vision which relate the *Stern der Erlösung* to *Being and Time*. The often brutally oxymoronic turns of language and of thought in Karl Barth, notably the dialectic of divine hiddenness and revelation, have their close correspondence in Heidegger on truth. In both texts a violent existentialism in reference to man's enigmatic "thrownness" into life accompanies an equally violent sense of illumination, of presence "behind" the extant. Ernst Bloch's use of *parataxis,* of anaphoric reiteration, has its parallels in Heidegger, as does the device of abstract personalization, the grammatical treatment of abstract and prepositional categories as if they were nominal presences. There is more than accidental echo as between Heidegger's portrayal of psychic decay and planetary waste in modernity and Spengler's *Menschendämmerung,* or "twilight of man." Heidegger's language, which is wholly inseparable from his philosophy and from the problems which that philosophy poses, must be seen as a characteristic phenomenon arising out of the circumstances of Germany between the cataclysm of 1918 and the rise to power of National Socialism. Many of the difficulties we experience in seeking to hear and interpret that language today stem directly from its untimeliness, from the fact that we bring to bear, inevitably, our awareness of history and of discourse as these developed in the 1940s and 1950s on an earlier speech-world.

Justly, Gadamer tells of Martin Heidegger's *Wortgenie,* of his "word-genius." Heidegger can sense and follow the etymological "arteries into the primal rock of language." The author of *Sein und Zeit,* of the lectures on the meaning of metaphysics, of the *Letter on Humanism,* of the commentaries on Nietzsche, on Hölderlin, or on Schelling, is, with Plato and with Nietzsche, a stylist of exceeding power. His punning — where "punning" is too feeble a designation for an uncanny receptivity to the fields of resonance, of consonance, of suppressed echo in phonetic and semantic units — has bred, to the point of parody, the poststructuralism and deconstructionism of today. Heidegger belongs to the history of language and of literature as much as he does to that of ontology, of phenomenological epistemology, or of aesthetics (perhaps more so). By any measure, the *corpus* is overwhelming. It will run to more than sixty volumes (of which we have, until now, only a part, and inadequately edited).

Yet this prodigality and textual strength are, themselves, paradoxical. They tend to obscure a central *orality* in Heidegger's teaching and concept of the enterprise of serious thought.

Witnesses, such as Löwith, as Gadamer, as Hannah Arendt, are of one voice in saying that those who did not hear Martin Heidegger lecture or conduct his seminars can have only an imperfect, even distorted notion of his purpose. It is the lectures, the seminars already prior to *Sein und Zeit,* which, in Marburg in the very early 1920s, came as a shock of revelation to colleagues and students. The "secret king of thought," as Arendt memorably called her master, acted through the spoken word. Gadamer characterizes the experience of hearing Heidegger as one of "*Einbruch und Umbruch,*" of "break-in and of [destructive-foundational] transformation." The rare recordings we have of the ageing Heidegger's voice and mode of speech retain their spell. Critics have referred to a kind of histrionic sorcery, masked as questioning simplicity. This charge has, we know, an ancient ring. And the Socratic motif is of utmost relevance. Socrates is, rules Heidegger, the "purest" of all Western thinkers; that purity is immediate to the fact "that he does not write." Plato's *Phaedrus* and the Platonic *VIIth Letter* express the primal contradiction between the serious pursuit of the *Logos*, of philosophic insight on the one hand, and writing on the other. The letter kills the spirit. The written text is mute in the face of responding challenge. It does not admit of inward growth and correction. Texts subvert the absolutely vital role of memory (Heidegger's key-term, *Erinnerung*). It is the sophist, the rhetorician, the venial orator who commit their craft to writing. The true poet is an oral rhapsode. The true thinker, the authentic pedagogue above all, relies on face-to-face speech, on the uniquely focused dynamics of direct address, as these knit question to answer, and living voice to living reception. This theme of the abstention from writing of all responsible philosophic teaching is perennial in the Western tradition (as it is also in the Orient). We find it in a sharp guise in the practices of Wittgenstein, himself, like Heidegger, an anti-academic academic and scorner of the "profession of philosophy" in its conventional and publicist sense. (It is, I believe, the conjunctions in depth between Wittgenstein and Heidegger, the two foremost philosophic-linguistic thinkers of the age, so seemingly antithetical, which offer the most fertile ground for coming investigation and comprehension.)

As we now know, the greater part of Heidegger's work lay unpublished. *Being and Time* remains incomplete and was issued in its massively fragmentary form against Heidegger's initial intent. The questioning construct, the definitional repetitions, the tautologies which inform Heidegger's texts are, frequently, those of the lecture-note, of the intervention in the seminar or of the dialogue. The fiction of such a dialogue, with a Japanese student, is enacted in one of Heidegger's major essays on the nature of language. I have found that passages in Heidegger which are opaque to the reading eye and stony on the page come to more intelligible life, take on a logic of an almost musical kind when they are read aloud, when one hears them read or spoken as did the students, the public audiences to which they were first articulated. To read Heidegger may, therefore, be in some sense not only a problematic but an unnatural proceeding.

But the question of whether Martin Heidegger is saying anything substantive and arguable *at all,* of whether his voluminous pronouncements upon man and *mundum* are anything but tautological incantations, lies even deeper. From Carnap to the present, analytic philosophy has treated *Sein und Zeit* and subsequent Heidegger-texts as "pure mystification," as "non-sense" of a peculiarly obscurantist and melodramatic sort. What is, to Gadamer, one of the principal "acts of disinterested thought" in the history of philosophy has been, most evidently in the Anglo-American climate of discourse, a fearsome example of the irrationalism, of the hypnotic deconstruction of logical argument, as these tide across German and, to some extent, French sensibility after Hegel and Nietzsche. Heidegger's politics are, in this reading, of a piece with the nocturnal vacancy and magisterial primitivity of his prose. I have, throughout this small book on Heidegger, sought to clarify the implications and scope of this fundamental critique; and I have, tentatively, pointed to what I take to be the underlying, the genetic origin of a very real dilemma. Let me come back to this hypothesis.

"I am a theologian," declares Martin Heidegger to those who, at Marburg and in the early years in Freiburg, sought guidance to the revolutionary nature of his style and teachings. Heidegger's training is theological. It is the inadequacy of the Thomist incorporation of Aristotle on "being" which instigates Heidegger's work on pseudo-Duns Scotus and those first seminars on Aristotle's *Rhetoric* which revealed a new presence in European thought. The letter to Karl Löwith, in the decisive year 1921, is explicit: "Do not measure me by the standards of any creative philosopher . . . I am a Christian theologian." From the outset, Heidegger's manner of questioning and defining, Heidegger's tactics of citation and of hermeneutic elucidation, intimately reflect the Scholastic and neo-Kantian theological techniques in which he had been trained. His early exemplars, those whom he studies and, initially, echoes, are St. Paul, St. Augustine, Kierkegaard, religious *illuminati* such as Eckhardt, and the German Pietists from whom Heidegger, like Hölderlin, derives some of his most audacious lexical and grammatical strokes. Above all, the Heideggerian determination to ask ultimate questions, his un-negotiated and non-negotiable postulate that serious human thought must dwell persistently on "first and last things" (it is here that the antinomies to the philosophy-world of Hume and of Frege are most drastic), have their inception and justification in a religious-theological sphere of values. If Martin Heidegger inquires, untiringly, of the being of Being, of *on* and *ousia*, it is because theology, and the theological uses of Aristotle, have directed him so to do.

It is during the actual composition of *Sein und Zeit* that there would seem to have occurred what I take to be the initial and radical *Kehre* ("turn") in Heidegger's stance. It is that from the theological to the ontological. We know Heidegger's fierce insistence on this dissociation. *Being and Time* and the works that followed disclaim any theological reference. They constitute an intransigent critique of transcendence in the theological and neo-Platonic sense.

Most stringently, Martin Heidegger rejects what he calls "the onto-theological"; this is to say the attempts to found a philosophy of being or epistemology of consciousness on some kind of rationally or intuitively postulated theological basis. The inference of any such basis, as we find it, capitally, in Kant or, more covertly, in the hypostasis of *Geist* (of "Spirit") in Hegel's teleological historicism, is, to Heidegger, wholly illicit. An authentic ontology, such as he develops it, is a "thinking of" human existential immanence whose referral to being, to the primordial, naked fact and truth of essence, has no theological dimension. Time and again, Heidegger makes this discrimination imperative to his enterprise and to our understanding of the human condition. Even more drastically than an "overcoming of metaphysics" (whose theological foundations, certainly in the Western tradition, are perennially transparent), Heidegger's thought is an "overcoming of theology" or, more precisely and crucially, a supersession of the theological ghosts which, obstinately, inhabit Western philosophy even in its most explicitly agnostic or atheist vein (that of Nietzsche). Heidegger's allusions to theology, to the uses which theologians in Marburg and elsewhere were making of his ontology, became increasingly ironic. The distance between himself and the theologians had to be made wholly unmistakable. In late years, he was wont to observe that the problem, on which he himself had no opinion, was not whether theology could be a *Wissenschaft* (a scientific, positive corpus of method and knowledge), but whether it had any right to be.

There is no reason to query Heidegger's convictions on this key issue. The perception that his anxiety for differentiation precisely expresses his own awareness of the close neighborhood of the theological to his ontological radicalism is legitimate. But it does not, *a priori*, refute Heidegger's claims to existential immanence, to the "thereness of the world" and of the phenomenality of the extant in a set of categories which are neither theological nor anti-theological, but entirely extraneous to the theological dimension (as are, comparably, the models of being in modern scientific cosmologies). The question is: what is the role in Heidegger's thought and language, these two being strictly inseparable, of the renunciation and refusal of the theological? Could there, in fact, be a communicable, an arguably intelligible, articulation of an ontology of pure immanence?

This, I believe, is *the* question to address to Heidegger's teachings. I advert to it in this book. But it needs to be urged more strongly.

The violence of neologism, of grammatical compaction in Heidegger's discourse materially reflects the endeavor, under persistent strain, to forge a language of ontological totality in which the theological presence would not intrude. The languages of mathematics and of formal logic are able to encode a systematic immanence. They need not refer to the transcendent, to the undefinable. They are, in a sense, dynamic tautologies. Paradoxically, there are analogies to this self-closure in Heidegger's idiom. The copula, the *is,* which, epistemologically and ontologically, constitutes the constant object of Martin Heidegger's meditation, also embodies the principal instrument of his style. *Sein und Zeit,* the lectures on metaphysics, on the act of thought, the expositions of Schelling and of Nietzsche, the later writings on art, abound in open and veiled tautologies. In the Heideggerian dialectic, A is defined as A in a tautological imperative which, consciously or not, generates a counter-statement to the tautological self-definition of the transcendent as it speaks out of the Burning Bush. The "I am what I am" or "I am that which is" of the Mosaic Deity is exactly counter-echoed in Heidegger's definitions of Being, *qua* Being, in his strenuous refusal to allow the definitional dispersal of Being in beings.

The intractable difficulty here is this: mathematics and symbolic logic can, indeed, proceed within systematic tautology and enclosure. Natural language, as we have inherited it from Hebraic and Hellenic sources, as it has, in the West, been indelibly marked by Platonic immateriality and by Judaeo-Christian transcendentalism, cannot be purged convincingly of its meta-physical register, connotations, and implicit inference. To speak after Scripture and the *Phaedrus*, after St. Augustine and Dante, after Kant and Dostoevsky, is to speak transcendentally. It is to use, even if involuntarily, fundamental categories of "other-dimensionality," be they theological, spiritual (also in a psychological sense), or mythological, where "mythology" stands for the Platonism and neo-Platonism which have so innervated the life of the mind and of the imagination in the West.

Martin Heidegger's counter-action has been formidable. It engages not only his own recasting of German philosophic speech. It animates his vexed and metamorphic translations from the pre-Socratics, from Aristotle, from the Latin of the Scholastics. Heidegger's readings and re-phrasings of Sophocles, of Hölderlin, of Trakl are attempts to reclaim for a language of ontological presentness, of *Gegenwart*, the high ground illicitly (according to Heidegger) occupied by the onto-theology and metaphysics which perpetuate our "forgetting of Being." They are, to use a celebrated Heidegger-trope, the labors of a woodcutter, seeking to hack out a path to the "clearing," to the luminous "thereness of what is."

I have argued that Heidegger's prodigious purgation (*katharsis*) is among the major acts in the history of thought and of language. Its challenge, its provocation and influence are, will be immense. But a sense of ultimate failure is difficult to deny. Notoriously, Heidegger himself was unable to arrive at a definition of *Sein*, of Being and the being of Being, that is not either a pure tautology or a metaphoric and infinitely regressive chain. He himself admitted this fact, attributing to human speech itself some radical inadequacy in the face of Being. There is a cardinal instability, indeed, contradiction at the very heart of Heidegger's undertaking. The 1943 afterword to *Was ist Metaphysik?* ("What Is Metaphysics?") propounds that "Being *wohl west* [a strictly untranslatable Heideggerian coinage signifying something like "is dynamically, breathes seminally"] without the extant, but that there can never be anything extant without Being" (*"das Sein wohl west ohne das Seiende, dass neimals aber ein Seiendes ist ohne das Sein"*). In the fifth edition of the lecture, this central doctrine is simply inverted. We are now told that *"das Sein nie ist ohne das Seiende"* ("there is never a being of Being without the extant"). Within six years the whole ontological postulate has been reversed. Gadamer justly infers the "eschatological pathos" which was unleashed upon Heidegger and Germany during these years. But the muddle does lie deeper. As everywhere else in Heidegger, the thought and speech-experiment which is demanded in order to "think Being" independent of extants, of that which actually and existentially is, proves abortive. Or, what matters far more, the experiment itself constitutes an involuntary reversion to the theological. Replace *Sein* by "God" in all the key passages and their meaning becomes pellucid. A *Sein ohne Seiendes* ("a Being without beings") such as Heidegger *must* postulate it if he is to remain true to the anti-metaphysics and anti-theology of his teachings, is inconceivable and unsayable in precisely the ways in which the *Deus absconditus*, the unmoved Prime Mover of Aristotelian and Augustinian transcendentalism, is inconceivable and unsayable.

The equivalence is that which Heidegger labors, almost desperately, to avoid. Again and again, his language and the claims to intelligibility of his definitions and translations break under the strain. Heidegger mines etymologies to unprecedented and frequently arbitrary depths. At the heart of the dark he finds, again, the ancient gods.

Hence the turn, itself inexhaustibly fascinating, to poetry, to the arts after what Heidegger himself seems to have recognized as a central defeat not only politically, but philosophically. In a motion which is almost that of Schelling and of philosophic aestheticism (in the wake of Nietzsche), Heidegger locates in the *mysterium tremendum* of the Hölderlin ode, of the Van Gogh painting, that "otherness" of absolute presence, of ontological self-signification, to which he cannot allow a theological-metaphysical status. Hence also, and most enigmatically, the turn toward "the gods," toward the *Geviert* ("foursome") of pagan, chthonic forces in Heidegger's last writings. For the later Heidegger, Being is presentness in the poetry, in the art we believe in. But how can that which "shines through" the choral song in *Antigone*, how can that which "conceals and discloses itself as the true being of Being" in Van Gogh's painting of peasant shoes, be thought, be said in terms other than those of transcendence? Words failed Heidegger and, at a pivotal stage in his life and work, he failed them. The symmetries of immanence are cruel.

II.

My introduction to Martin Heidegger first appeared in 1978. By that date it was entirely possible to arrive at a general picture of Heidegger's involvement in National Socialism. Guido Schneeberger's *Nachlese zu Heidegger*, published in 1962, contained the essential texts. Here one could find the ultra-nationalist and pro-Nazi public pronouncements made by Heidegger during his *Rektorat* at the University of Freiburg in Breisgau. Nine years before, Karl Löwith's poignant, incisive *Heidegger: Denker in dürftiger Zeit* had set out the central paradox of the co-existence in Heidegger of a philosopher of towering stature and of an active partisan in barbarism. Further elements of the case were contributed by Karl Jaspers's *Notizen zu Martin Heidegger* (1978) and the expanded edition of Jaspers's *Philosophische Autobiographie* which had appeared the year previous. A largely apologetic view of the matter was available in Otto Pöggeler's study: *Philosophie und Politik bei Heidegger* of 1972. Above all, any interested reader could consult the crucial interview with Heidegger, an interview intolerably shrewd and evasive, published posthumously in the *Spiegel* in 1966. This text alone ought to have focused attention on the theme of Heidegger's near-total silence about the Holocaust during the years of his teaching and writing after 1945. It is this silence and the one notorious sentence which breaks it — a sentence in which Heidegger equates Auschwitz with the practice of battery-farming and with the nuclear threat — that, to my mind, constitutes the *gravamen* of the whole tragic affair. So far as I am aware, my own little book was among the very first, if not indeed the first, to state that it is Heidegger's silence post-1945 rather than the opaque and pathetic rhetoric of 1933–34 which challenges our understanding.

From 1984 onward, the articles of Hugo Ott have provided an invaluable, detailed examination of Heidegger's activities as *Rektor,* of his attitude toward colleagues and students, and of his relations to the regime in Berlin (these several articles are now gathered in Ott's *Martin Heidegger: Unterwegs zu seiner Biographie,* 1988). Löwith's calm but devastating indictment of Heidegger's comportment and views in the mid-1930s had become available in *Mein Leben in Deutschland vor und nach 1933* (1986). Numerous aspects of Heidegger's political, pragmatic role and significance are touched upon in *Heidegger und die praktische Philosophie* (edited by Pöggeler and by

Annemarie Gethmann-Siefert, 1988). But it is, undeniably, the publication in October 1987 of the French version of Victor Farias's *Heidegger et le nazisme* which unleashed the storm. Since that date, the polemic literature has assumed almost grotesque volume. Books, articles, special numbers of philosophic-political journals, have poured in. There are now monographic surveys and bibliographies of this debate. Matters have been made murkier and more acrimonious by the posthumous publication of certain anti-semitic, pro-Germanic articles written by the young Paul De Man. There *are* contiguities, although of an exceedingly subtle kind, with the Heidegger *fracas*. It has, over the past few years, been almost impossible to keep up with the tumult of voices, accusing or apologetic, humanist or deconstructive. The Heidegger cause is now all too *célèbre*.

This is somewhat odd. Farias's book is, where it touches on philosophy, of the utmost vulgarity and imprecision. It is, moreover, crammed with *errata* not only in regard to facts and dates but in its translations from Heidegger (some of these have been listed in Thomas Sheehan's article on "Heidegger and the Nazis," in the *New York Review of Books* for June 16, 1988, pp. 38–39). Very little in Farias was not previously available in the research of Ott or in such testimony as that of Wilhelm Schoeppe on Heidegger and Baumgarten published in the *Frankfurter Allgemeine Zeitung* (May 28, 1983). None the less, it is true that Farias's work has a cumulative impact. The sheer assemblage of documents and eyewitness reports, notably for the period 1933–45, is impressive. Somber nuggets have been dug out. Farias has shown Heidegger to be lying when he sought to conceal his retention until 1945 of his membership card in the Nazi Party. He has clarified the full extent of Heidegger's psychic collapse after the surrender of the Reich and shown how patently inadequate were the answers which Martin Heidegger gave to those who, during the time of the denazification tribunals, investigated his conduct. Owing to Farias's excavations, unscholarly and virulently selective as these often are, specific moments in Heidegger's abject treatment of endangered academic colleagues, in Heidegger's admiration for the Führer, and in Heidegger's cunning tactics of survival, can no longer be passed over. But, like so many before him and even now, Farias fails to say anything substantive as to the possible congruence between the ontology of *Sein und Zeit* and the rise of Nazism. Nor does he perceive the enormity of Heidegger's post-war silence, of the refusal by the philosopher of Being, by the master-reader of Sophocles and of Hölderlin, to address his conscience, his reflection, his discourse to the inhuman negation of life in which he had played a part (however rhetorical, however mandarin).

Being and Time is written during the early 1920s. It comes, as I have said, of the apocalypse of 1918 and of the Expressionist climate. It fully predates National Socialism. No Nazi hoodlum, to my knowledge, ever read or would have been capable of reading it. The crux, made more complex by the problem of Deconstruction and of such post-Heideggerians as De Man, is this: are there in Heidegger's incomplete ontological *summa* categories, advocacies of inhumanism, eradications of the human person, which, in some sense, prepare for the subsequent program of Nazism? Is Heidegger's play with and on Nothingness (a play intimately analogous with negative theology) a nihilism *in extremis* rather than, as it professes to be, an "overcoming of nihilism"? Assuredly, *Sein und Zeit* and Heidegger's theory of a language that speaks man rather than being spoken by him is utterly seminal in the modern anti-humanistic movement. There is little in Deconstruction or in Foucault's "abolition of man," with its background in Dada and Artaud, which is not voiced in Heidegger's *a*-humanism — where the *privativum* of the prefix does seem to me more accurate and just than would be that of *in*-humanism. Secondly, there is the famous urgency of death, of the will to and motion toward death in Heidegger's analysis of felt being, of human individuation. Rooted in Pascal and in Kierkegaard, this death-insistence does, by virtue of the fact that it attempts to free itself from theological contexts, carry a heavy charge of negation. Can we say that this weight inflects Heidegger's and his reader's attitudes toward the macabre obsessions of National Socialism?

I see no ready answer to either of these questions. *Post hoc* is not *propter hoc.* Books of the difficulty and singularity of *Sein und Zeit* do not, in any immediate or programmatic way, exercise their effect upon politics and society. It may indeed be the case that Heidegger's tonality, that Heidegger's charismatic regency of certain circles of intellect and of sensibility in the Germany of the late 1920s and early 1930s did contribute to the ambience of fatality and of dramatization in which Nazism flourished. Intuitively, such a conjunction seems plausible. But it could only be demonstrated if specific texts in Heidegger's *magnum* could be shown to have generated dependent motions of argument and of action in Hitler's rise to power. No such demonstration has, despite attempts by such critics of Heidegger as Adorno and Habermas, carried conviction. It could well be that we stand too near the facts. Darkness can blind as sharply as light; and the two may take centuries to untangle (consider the debates which persist over the politics and the impact on politics of Machiavelli or of Rousseau).

What strikes me as perfectly evident is the extent of Heidegger's rhetorical and administrative participation in the Nazification of the German university-world in 1933–34.

Like so many other intellectuals, Heidegger was manifestly caught up in the brutal, festive inebriation which swept across Germany after some fifteen years of national humiliation and despair. Naked power can mesmerize the academic-mandarin temper (Sigmund Freud was, for a spell, entranced by Mussolini, and those thinkers and writers who worshipped at Stalin's shrine were legion). Unquestionably, Martin Heidegger saw himself as a chosen *praeceptor Germaniae,* as a leader-in-thought who would mold a national resurrection. The Platonic image, not only in reference to Plato's doctrines of philosophic governance but also with regard to Plato's role as adviser to Sicilian despotism, lay to hand. The chapter of the unwisdom of philosophers in regard to matters political is a long one. Voltaire's Jew-hatred was rabid. The racism of Frege was of the blackest hue. Sartre not only sought to evade or find apologia for the world of the Gulag; he deliberately falsified what he knew of the insensate savagery of the Cultural Revolution in Maoist China. It is an ill-kept secret that cloistered intellectuals and men who spend their lives immured in words, in texts, can experience with especial intensity the seductions of violent political proposals, most particularly where such violence does not touch their own person. There can be in the sensibility and outlook of the charismatic teacher, of the philosophical absolutist, more than a touch of surrogate sadism (Ionesco's *Lesson* is a macabre parable on this condition).

These precedents and psychological data are no apologia. Martin Heidegger's *Rektoratsrede,* his notorious address in support of Hitler's break with the League of Nations, his elegy on a nationalist thug who the French occupying authorities executed in the Rhineland and of whom the Nazis made a martyr, are nauseating documents. They breathe the infatuation with ferocity and mystique of a small man abruptly transported (or, rather, thinking himself transported) to the hub of great political-historical affairs. I find nothing more painful, more perplexing in the clamorous wake of the Farias book than the resolve by certain eminent spirits to salvage precisely *these* lamentable texts. In Derrida's *De l'esprit: Heidegger et la question,* in Lacoue-Labarthe's *L'imitation des modernes* and *La fiction du politique,* we find a voluminous, minutely-argued plea for their high centrality in Heidegger, indeed in all modern political-pedagogic reflection. Comparison of the *Rektoratsrede* with Plato's *VIIth Letter,* with Hobbes or Rousseau, is pervasive. Affinities are teased out as between the opaque, bathetic rhetoric of Heidegger's 1933–34 speeches and articles and the vocabulary of his pre-eminent writings on ontology, metaphysics, and the arts. If we are to believe the masters of French Deconstruction — who, very rightly and properly, do see in Heidegger the begetter of the whole Deconstructionist hermeneutic — the *Rektoratsrede* constitutes nothing less than a fundamental revaluation of the role of thought and of education in the modern state, and its significance in reference to such concepts as "consciousness" and "destiny" is of the utmost. To believe this one must, I venture, be tone-deaf to the inflated brutality, to the macabre *Kitsch* in Heidegger's language and syntax at this point (translation into French, etymologizing recession toward Kant and even Aristotle, as practiced by Derrida, by Lacoue-Labarthe, by Lyotard, masks the true nature of the original). No less than, say, some of Bertrand Russell's pontifications on the United States, Heidegger's academic-bureaucratic pronouncements during and immediately after Hitler's assumption of power constitute a no doubt significant, a no doubt problematic, but also fundamentally aberrant phenomenon. This *erratum* has been ill served by its exegetes.

Once more: the disabling fact is Heidegger's silence

after 1945. This appalling abstention is contemporaneous with some of his most far-reaching work in reference to the nature of planetary-ecological crises, in reference to the nature of language and of the arts. Martin Heidegger is working and lecturing at the peak of his powers during the very years in which he refuses all response to the question of the true quality of Hitlerism and of the Auschwitz consequence. Notoriously, in 1953, he reprints unaltered the celebrated sentence in the foreword of "What Is Metaphysics?" in which the "unrealized" or hidden verity of National Socialism was first invoked. Then there is the one other sentence which I have already cited. Otherwise *silentium*. Heidegger does not, during the 1950s and 1960s, fail to pronounce on the American-Russian hegemony over the planet; on the destruction of the environment (which he had already, and with superb clairvoyance, adverted to in the 1920s). As we know from the *Spiegel* interview, he was preparing a peculiarly mendacious posthumous apologia for his own role in the 1930s and 1940s. But the thinker of Being found nothing to say of the Holocaust and the death-camps.

In my introductory study, I suggested that this vacuum might have risen from Heidegger's specific vision of German destiny or "mittance" (*Schickung*), from his conviction that Germany and the German language, which he held to be comparable only to ancient Greek, were destined, were "called upon," to manifest, to experience both the very apex of human accomplishment — in German philosophy, in the music of the German-speaking world, in the poetry of Hölderlin — and the very abyss. To judge of the catastrophe of Auschwitz would be, in some ineluctable argument on symmetry, to put in question the ontological-historical singularity and pre-eminence of the fate of "Germanity." I still believe that there may be truth or, at the least, a contribution to truth in this suggestion.

But it no longer seems at all sufficient. And it is an un-doubted merit of Farias's attainder and of the debate which has ensued, that the problem of Heidegger's mute-ness after the end of the Reich and his own adroitly-managed restoration to authority, has become blindingly central.

Numerous answers have been forthcoming. Anti-Heideggerians have proclaimed flatly that the tenebrous, finally indecipherable ontology of *Sein und Zeit* has been exposed once and for all by the root incapacity of Heideg-ger to "think Auschwitz," to see in what ways the bestial-ity of Nazism can be situated in a rational understanding of social and political history. Heidegger's silence after 1945 would, in essence, deconstruct the claims of his phi-losophy to any serious insights into the human condition and into the relations between consciousness and action. A more qualified view is that which bears on Heidegger's *Kehre,* the arguable "turn" from the ontology of *Being and Time* to the evacuation of man from thought, from speech, from art and the interplay of "the earth and the gods" in his later works. In the pure, cold light of that reading of essence, political history, even of an apocalyptic tenor, would, strictly regarded, be immaterial, be extraneous to any rigorous "thinking of Being." More subtly, proponents of Heidegger have advanced the idea that the technology of the Nazi extermination-process, of the Soviet Gulag, of the nuclear armaments, emphatically fulfills Heidegger's prophetic analysis of the — nihilistic — technocratic de-cay of man's present-in-the-world. Heidegger had been *too right.* For him to say so in the post-war climate was sheerly impossible. Any validating self-citation would have been more scandalous than silence. Chillingly, Lyotard, in his *Heidegger et les "juifs"* (1988), suggests that Ausch-witz enacted, to a supreme degree, that "forgetting of Being" which lies at the heart of Heidegger's analysis of

Western history and consciousness. Within that dominant context, the "forgetting of the Jews" (annihilation being a final tautology for non-remembrance) would have been the perfectly logical, foreseeable product. Heidegger did not need to articulate that terrible truth which, to the perceptive reader, was wholly latent in his phenomenology of the existential.

There are those who urge patience, who point, with some justification, to the incompleteness of the evidence. So much of Heidegger's writings, teaching, correspondence is, as yet, inaccessible. Documents to come may throw decisive light on Heidegger's options and decisions after the war. Some pivotal and humanely acceptable dictum may yet emerge from the voluminous *Nachlass*. Finally, there are apologists for Martin Heidegger, though few, to whom the great silence of the Master signifies a profound decency and *dignitas*. If I sense rightly the attitude toward Heidegger of the great poet and Resistance-fighter René Char or of an admirer such as Braque, it points in this direction. What *could* Heidegger have said? What except opportunistic banalities could the language of Hölderlin, of Kant, of Heidegger himself have to offer on the matter of ultimate bestiality and self-destruction? What philosopher, *anywhere*, has had anything but more or less vacuous platitudes to say of the night which came upon man in the 1940s?

The mere intricacy and possibility of overlap between these several attempts at explication suggest that there must be some pertinence among them. To which can be added the possibility (I do think it is more than that) that Heidegger was, in *propria persona*, a small character, an ageing man haunted by ruse, by ambition, by certain deeply-incised and "agrarian" traditions of concealment and exploitation. His acre of ground might have seen the harvest of Hell, but it was his.

Paul Celan is important in a profile of Heidegger, and the theme of the relations between Celan and Heidegger has become crucial to our vision of Heidegger's influence, and more particularly in regard to his stance after 1945. The very few scholars (Bernard Böschenstein preeminently among them) who have had access to Celan's library and private notes testify to the constant intensity of the poet's preoccupation with Heidegger's works. It would appear that Celan annotated *Sein und Zeit* in minute detail and that he knew intimately Heidegger's readings of Hölderlin, George, and Trakl. What is absolutely clear is the degree to which Paul Celan's radically innovative vocabulary and, at certain points, syntax are Heideggerian. No doubt, there is often a shared provenance: in baroque and Pietist German idiom, in Hölderlin, above all in Rilke, whose linguistic influence on both Heidegger and Celan was extensive. Nevertheless, it is of Heidegger's very name that Paul Celan welds a vivid marker. It is *"heidegängerisch"* that the poet moves (the adjectival pun, with its play on "heath" and on "going" or "walking," is not only untranslatable, but plays back toward Heidegger's own registration of both "heath" and "acre" in his name). It is the *"heidegängerisch Nähe"* (that which "is close in its heath-walk which is Heidegger's") that Celan turns to in "Largo," one of his most densely allusive and self-allusive lyrics. Martin Heidegger, in turn, was observant of Celan's poetry and, a rare public act, attended Celan's readings. Even on the basis of incomplete documentation, the intensity and depth of the inward relationship is palpable.

Together with Primo Levi (and both men chose suicide at the height of their strengths), Paul Celan is the *only* survivor of the Holocaust whose writings are, in some true degree, commensurate with the unspeakable. Only in Levi and Celan does language, in the exact face of sub-human yet all too human enormity and finality, retain its

reticent totality. The Auschwitz-fact, the massacre of European Jews at German hands, permeates the entirety of
Celan's work and life. Thus, even on a purely intellectual
plane, the turn of Celan toward Heidegger would be problematic. But this turn was, as we know, far more than abstract. The two men were present to each other with a rare
force. The crystallization of that reciprocal presentness was
Celan's visit to Heidegger's famous hut at Todtnauberg
a few years before Celan's suicide. That visit and the sole
known witness to it, the poem entitled "Todtnauberg,"
published in *Lichtzwang* in 1970, have become the object
of fervid inquiry and speculation. An hermeneutic mythology has mushroomed around a central opacity. Both
Derrida and Lacoue-Labarthe have devoted monographic
treatment, at once poignant and fine-spun, to the lyric and
to the complexities of meaning from which it sprang. Of
the encounter we know only what Celan's enigmatic recall
tells us or, rather, elects not to tell us. That there came
to pass a numbing, soul-lacerating deception — in the
etymological senses of that word which signifies both "dis-
appointment" and "falsehood" — is unmistakable. As
"through a glass darkly," and darker than darkly, we sense
in "Todtnauberg" a dread silence. Celan came to question,
to "put in question" Heidegger's perception or non-percep-
tion of the *Shoah*, of the "death-winds" that had made ash
of millions of human beings and of the Jewish legacy
which informed Celan's destiny. If any individual had the
right, the obligation to ask for some answer, be it that of
impotent desolation, to the question of the inhuman, it
was Paul Celan. When he wrote, as he did, his name in
Heidegger's visitor's book, Celan was taking the risk of an
ultimate trust in the possibility of encounter, of the renascence of the word out of a shared night. So far as we know,
to the extent that "Todtnauberg" instructs us, that trust
was violated either by trivial evasion (as in the *Spiegel-*

interview) or by utter silence, by a complete abstention from discourse such as Heidegger resorted to also in pedagogic situations. Either way, the effect on Celan can be felt to have been calamitous. But the issue far transcends the personal. Throughout his writings and teachings, Martin Heidegger had proclaimed the deed of questioning to be of the essence; he had defined the question as the piety of the human spirit. Whatever happened at Todtnauberg, when the foremost poet in the language after Hölderlin and Rilke sought out the "secret king of thought," blasphemed against Heidegger's own cardinal sense of the holiness of asking. It may, for our epoch at least, have made irreparable the breach between human need and speculative thought, between the music of thought that is philosophy and that of being which is poetry. Much in Western consciousness has its instauration in the banishment of the poets from the Platonic city. In somber counterpoint, Heidegger's denial of reply to Celan and the poem which resulted amount to a banishment, to a self-ostracism of the philosopher from the city of man.

One further analysis of Heidegger's abstention in reference to 1933–45 may be worth testing. Heideggerian thought is prodigal of epistemological, phenomenological, aesthetic insights. It invites a revaluation of certain aspects of Aristotelian and Scholastic logic and rhetoric. It is, self-professedly, the most comprehensive argument we have on ontology, on the facticity of the existential. But it neither contains nor implies any ethics. Heidegger was, himself, peremptory on this point. He wholly repudiated attempts, notably by the Marburg theologians and by certain humanist-existentialists in France, to derive any ethical principles or methodologies from his works. He defined ethics such, for example, as we find them in Kant and such as we can legitimately infer them from Hegelian historicism, as being altogether extrinsic to his own strictly ontological enterprise. The "thinking of Being" is of an order totally other than the prescriptive, normative, or heuristic "thinking of conduct." In the massive, reiterative body of Heidegger's writings, the signal absence is very precisely that of the concept of evil (except in so far as we may construe the spoliation of the natural world to constitute a radical negativity). Far beyond Nietzsche, Heidegger thinks, feels in categories *outside* good and evil. Heidegger's precept and image whereby death is a "shrine" in which Being is most nakedly, most epiphanically present, categorically sublates (the dialectical *Aufhebung*) the problem of good and evil as this problem attaches to metaphysics in traditional systems of thought. Had Heidegger sought the understanding of the evil of Nazism and of his role therein, had he striven to "think Auschwitz" at anything near the requisite depth (and what philosopher has done so?), the domain of the ethical would have been indispensable. It is, I venture, this domain which he had, in his renunciation of theology, excluded, and that exclusion crippled his humanity.

Lacking an ethic, self-maimed in the face of the inhuman, Heidegger's ontology remains an overwhelming fragment (as, explicitly, does *Sein und Zeit*). For all its actual dimensions — few philosophers have written or lectured more voluminously — Heidegger's work does resemble the fragmentary, often esoteric method of his beloved pre-Socratics. Even the most prolix, patient, discursive movements in Heidegger have something of the Heraclitean quality of the sudden illumination, of the "lightning which gathers" (Heidegger's disputed reading of a simile in Heraclites). What blazes in Heidegger at his best is a slow lightning. Heidegger would have been the first to underline the fragmentary, preliminary nature of his labors. He conceived these to be no more than a didactic, purgative preparation for a revolution in thought and in sensibility yet to come. Our incapacity, Heidegger's incapacity, to articulate Being in any systematically intelligible manner tells of the transitional, tragically splintered tenor of modernity. Like Hölderlin, like Nietzsche, and in constant reference to them, Heidegger is literally haunted by intimations of a revolutionary return to the source, of a homeward circling (comparable to that in the poetry and apocalyptic theosophy of Yeats). There will be "new gods" and only their coming, at our midnight, can save us. This notion of "salvation" (*Rettung*) pulses throughout Heidegger's teachings after the decisive advertence to Hölderlin and to Nietzsche during the 1940s. It becomes explicitly mythologized in the later texts on art. It was as if the *Feldweg*, the forest-path and fire-break which Heidegger used as a talismanic image of the thinker's journey, led back to some of the crucial *Lichtungen* ("clearings") in the soteriology, in the theological proposals of salvation, which the young Martin Heidegger had striven to reject. In the final analysis, the *Logos* proclaimed by Heidegger, the Word through which Being *is,* is like a valedictory twin of the *Logos* which speaks dawn in the Johannine Gospel. It was, as for so many master spirits and makers in our age of the "afterword," not new gods who were waiting at the crossroads, but the old God in all his unacceptable durance. Heidegger wrestled against that meeting. The vehemence of that bout is the measure of his stature. And of his defeat, as a thinker, as a human person.

But that, surely, is the point. The only temporality, the only language adequate to Heidegger's purpose would be exactly that defined by Celan: "*im Norden der Zukunft*" ("to the north of the future"). Only there can the walker in the Black Forest and the singer of the almond tree, of the *Mandelbaum* and *Mandelstamm* which had flowered into Celan's only hope, meet again.

omnia praeclara tam difficilia quam rara sunt
all things excellent are as difficult as they are rare
—Spinoza, *Ethics*, v, 42

In Place of a Foreword

There are reasons, perhaps decisive, for not attempting a brief introduction to the thought of Martin Heidegger (1889–1976).

The first is material. The books, essays, and lectures that Heidegger published during the period of his activity from 1912 to 1970 are of considerable mass. They will make up sixteen volumes in the forthcoming complete edition of his works. But they constitute only a part of a much larger whole. The collected texts, the *Gesamtausgabe*, are expected to comprise fifty-seven volumes. Of these, only two have so far appeared: *Logik* (*Aristoteles*), the lectures on Aristotelian logic that Heidegger gave at the University of Marburg in the winter term of 1925–26, and *Die Grundprobleme der Phänomenologie*, the lectures for the summer term of 1927 on the fundamental or "foundational" problems of phenomenology. In the collected works, these will be volumes 21 and 24 respectively.

In other words, slightly less than one-third of Martin Heidegger's output is now available in anything like a definitive form. Granted that Heidegger's principal achievement, the monumental *Sein und Zeit* of 1927 (rendered into English by John Macquarrie and Edward Robinson: *Being and Time*, 1962), is in hand. So, as well, are such crucial statements as the monograph of 1929 on *Kant und das Problem der Metaphysik* (translated by James Churchill, 1962); the *Vom Wesen der Wahrheit* of 1933–34, which has appeared in a translation by R. F. C. Hull and Alan Crick in a collection entitled *Existence and Being* (1949); the key *Einführung in die Metaphysik*, based on a course of lectures given in the summer of 1935 (*Introduction to Metaphysics*, translated by Ralph Manheim, 1959); as well as a number of the essays on language, poetry, and the nature of thought composed from the 1930s to 1970 (a selection from which is translated by Albert Hofstadter in *Poetry, Language, Thought*, 1971). Nevertheless, works that may be of comparable intrinsic importance and that, quite obviously, are essential to an understanding of Heidegger's development are as yet unpublished. They include Heidegger's teaching on Fichte and Schelling and on Hegel's concept of negation; the 1924 treatise on the notion of time; the text on the meaning of "the beginning" and the primal (*Über den Anfang*), which dates from 1941; the winter 1942–43 lectures on Parmenides; the historical survey of metaphysics from Thomas Aquinas to Kant which Heidegger set out for his students in 1926–27; the treatment of Leibniz and logic in the year following; the 1946–48 analyses of the essence of nihilism; the considerations on "the history of being" (*Aus der Geschichte des Seyns*, 1939); and much else.

This means, quite simply, that any account of or

judgment on Heidegger's thought must, at present, be provisional. It is likely to be subject to qualification or rejection, even on essential points, once the unpublished works have appeared. It means, furthermore, that nothing very confident can be argued with regard to at least two of the most vexed topics in the whole study of Heidegger's accomplishment: the debate on whether or not there occurs a fundamental change or "turn" (*Kehre*) between the author of *Being and Time* and the later Heidegger—a turn that many interpreters locate in the *Introduction to Metaphysics*—and the even sharper controversies on Heidegger's implication in Nazism. Lacking as we do the texts of much of Heidegger's teaching in the mid-1930s and then again in the 1940s, we can deal with these two pivotal issues only tentatively. Thus the question of precisely what it was that Professor Heidegger taught in Freiburg concerning Nietzsche and the pre-Socratics during the university terms of 1940–44 is at once crucial and, as yet, answerable only in part. In short: the hope of saying anything conclusive—or, indeed, fully responsible on the sum of Heidegger's presence and performance—is premature. The *Gesamtausgabe* may not be ready until the 1990s.

The second reason is one of status. The history of thought is dense with disagreements and re-evaluations. Because all philosophic thought rethinks and creates for itself a precedent, for uses either of authority or of refutation, the status of different philosophers and philosophic schools alters and is perennially arguable. There are as many "Platos" as there are metaphysics, epistemologies, and political positions. (Does Sir Karl Popper's Plato designate the same figure as Rousseau's or Gilbert Ryle's?) How alive or how dead—the two are not exactly the same question—is Aquinian scholasticism in twentieth-century logic? Or consider the successive, radically antagonistic readings of Nietzsche from the 1920s to the present. But in each of these cases, there is broad consensus as to stature. Both Popper and Ryle concur as to Plato's paramount importance; Aquinas's relevance may be questioned, not the fineness and energy of his systematic discourse; even where Nietzsche is concerned—and here polemics are often uncompromising—the genius of the work, be it for good or evil, is assumed. Why else bother to re-examine and disagree?

The situation of Martin Heidegger is entirely different and, as far as I am aware, unique. Many philosophers would say that he is not a serious philosopher at all (Bertrand Russell's *History of Western Philosophy*, a vulgar but representative book, omits any mention of Heidegger). Some philosophers might allow that Heidegger is another sort of creature altogether—a "language-mystic," a "meta-theologian," an ominous symptom of the moral and intellectual disarray of our time. Yet others would rule that even a polemical discussion of Heidegger's case is merely futile. His writings are a thicket of impenetrable verbiage; the questions he poses are sham questions; the doctrines he puts forward are, so far as anything at all can be made of them, either false or trivial. To try to analyze Heideggerian "ontology," the study and theory of the nature of being or existence, is to speak, or to speak of, nonsense—non-sense, in the most drastic connotations of the term. The influence that Heidegger exercises on those who peer into the nebulous vortex of his rhetoric is nothing less than disastrous, both philosophically and politically.

The contrary view holds Martin Heidegger to be not only the most eminent philosopher or critic of metaphysics since Immanuel Kant but one of that small number of decisive Western thinkers which would include Plato, Aristotle, Descartes, Leibniz, and Hegel. The secondary literature on Heidegger now exceeds three thousand entries. These deal both with central topics in Heidegger's work—his philosophy of existence and the meaning of time, his radical revision of Platonic, Aristotelian, and Kantian models of truth and of logic, his theory of art, his meditations on technology, his language-scheme—and with the impact of Heidegger's thought on a bewildering diversity of disciplines and modern attitudes. There is a post-Heideggerian theology of which Rudolf Bultmann was but the first of a continuing series of representatives. The existentialism of Jean-Paul Sartre is, explicitly, a version and variant of the idiom and propositions in *Sein und Zeit.* Heidegger's explications of Heraclitus, Anaximander, Parmenides, Plato, and Aristotle have entered, though in a bitterly contested guise, into the whole current image of Greek thought and civilization. There is now a Heideggerian linguistics or "metaphysical etymologizing and nominalism"—again both highly controversial and formative. The "structuralist" and "hermeneutic" schools of textual interpretation (where "hermeneutic" signifies "the understanding of understanding," the attempt to formalize and describe from within the ways in which we interpret the meanings of meaning) draw copiously on Heidegger, via Hans-Georg Gadamer in Germany and Jacques Derrida in France. Even more arrestingly, Heidegger's doctrines on the nature of language and poetry have marked literary theory in Germany, in France, in the United States, where the current debate over the "nature of a literary text," over the dialectical interactions between poet, reader, and language are thoroughly Heideggerian. Indeed, they have had their impact on the actual practice of such poets as René Char and Paul Celan. It is now beginning to look as if Mallarmé and Heidegger are the two seminal figures in the current linguistic self-consciousness or "reflexivity" in literature and criticism.

At the time of Heidegger's death, on May 26, 1976, a number of French philosophers affirmed that in the domain of the spirit our century would be that of Heidegger, as the seventeenth century could be said to be that of Descartes and of Newton. Or as Hannah Arendt, herself a distinguished thinker on politics and the history of ideas, expressed it: throughout twentieth-century philosophic sensibility, Martin Heidegger has been "the secret king of thought." (I will come back to this notion of "secrecy.")

How can such extremity of disagreement arise? How is it possible for witnesses of comparable acuity and integrity to arrive at the antithetical conclusions that Heidegger is a prolix charlatan and poisoner of good sense or, on the contrary, a master of insight, a philosopher-teacher whose works may renew the inward condition of man? And is there not a special trap, of evasion or facility, in seeking a middle position in such debate? Let me repeat: there seems to be no other example of so absolute a difference of judgment in the whole range of the history of Western thought since Socrates.

The explanation, together with a third reason for not writing this little book, lies, I believe, with Heidegger's medium. To a greater or lesser degree, every significant writer or thinker hammers out a personal style. In philosophy, the role of style is central but also ambiguous. Very roughly, there are three main approaches. The philosopher can advance his arguments on, say, the nature of reality or the status of consciousness or the existence of moral imperatives in the most direct possible language, in the everyday idiom of his community. This would be the case with Descartes, with Hume, and, in a special self-conscious way, with the later Wittgenstein. Or he can expound his views in and via a novel vocabulary, making of the composition or redefinition of terms and grammatical forms the particular instrument of his doctrine. As far as we can tell, there is a distinctive Aristotelian terminology, itself translated and redefined in the language of the Thomists. In important respects, Hegelian logic and epistemology—that branch of philosophy which concerns the ways in which we know—are creators of their own vocabulary. So, to cite a modern instance, is the phenomenology devised by Heidegger's teacher and predecessor at Freiburg, Edmund Husserl. There is a third approach. The philosopher can make of language itself the complete or major focus of his investigation. He can inquire into what is meant by what is said, into the modes through which syntax either generates or constrains the possibilities of cognition. He can try to elucidate, to schematize the relations, be they concordant or independently creative, between the words and sentences we speak and our picture of the internal and external facts of experience. He may find that he has to construct a special "meta-language" in order to gain a vantage point for his inquiry. This third approach has been predominant in Anglo-American philosophy since the turn of the century.

Heidegger, whose first writings concern themselves with the vocabulary and corresponding logical and ontological categories of Duns Scotus and the medieval schoolmen (these texts are gathered in the *Frühe Schriften,* 1972), has been immersed in the "language-condition" of all human thought and existence to a deeper degree, perhaps, than any other philosopher. In *Sein und Zeit,* there is a deliberate enforcement of common, nontechnical speech, a determination that causes a characteristic stress and even violence of feeling to arrive at the roots of man and of man's being in the world, through the compaction, through the condensation of simple words into primal nodes of truth. Already in *Sein und Zeit,* Heidegger etymologizes. The simple word, the antique vulgate will serve precisely because it contains (according to Heidegger) the greatest charge of initial and valid human perception. Thus the old and plain words are the richest in sense. It is we who have forgotten their fundamental incisiveness and existential witness. By pondering intensely, and with a sort of vehement probing, the etymology and early history of a word, the thinker can compel it to yield its formidable quantum of illumination and energy. In *Sein und Zeit,* therefore, and from this book onward, Heidegger's seeming lapidary plainness, his use of short sentences—so contrastive with the style of German idealist philosophy from Kant to Schopenhauer—in effect masks a fiercely personal and intentionally "delaying" or even "blockading" idiom. We are to be slowed down, bewildered, and barred in our reading so that we may be driven deep.

But soon this etymologizing or uprooting of German and Greek words (we shall see that Heidegger assigns to these two languages a strictly incomparable status) becomes much more than an instrument. It is made the cardinal move in Heideggerian philosophy. One takes a common locution, or a passage in Heraclitus, in Kant, in Nietzsche. One excavates from individual syllables, words, or phrases their original, long-buried, or eroded wealth of meaning. One demonstrates that the occlusion of this meaning has altered and damaged the destiny of Western thought, and how its rediscovery, its literal restoration to active radiance, can bring on a renascence of intellectual and moral possibility. Inevitably, this mining of language in general and of the language of previous philosophers in particular feeds back into Heidegger's own parlance.

From the mid-1930s on, Heideggerian German becomes a conscious, immediately recognizable apartness. When using words in what seem totally arbitrary ways, when welding words into uncouth chains of hyphenation, Heidegger claims that he is, in fact, returning to the wellsprings of language, that he is realizing the authentic intentions of human discourse. Whether or not this claim is defensible is a point I must come back to. But the effect is certain: a Heideggerian text is often strange and impenetrable beyond that of even the most difficult of preceding metaphysicians and mystics. In the late Heidegger, and under the impact of the poetry of Friedrich Hölderlin, language enters on an even more extreme stage of singularity. Words are now used partly in their own, supposedly primal and radical sense, and partly in a field of connotation and metaphor unique to Heidegger. The words themselves are almost always "simple." But the meanings that Heidegger attaches to "gods," "mortals," "sky," and "earth" (the famous *Geviert*, or "foursome," of the essays on thought and poetry, on *Denken und Dichten*, written between 1941 and 1947) are almost wholly idiosyncratic. Heidegger's philosophic speech becomes what linguists call an "idiolect," the idiom of an individual. But in this case the individual aims to give to his private style of communication a universal bearing. Heidegger is perfectly aware of the implicit affront and paradoxicality of this proceeding. We shall see how he justifies it. Whether or not one accepts this justification, the result is the same: no aspect of Heideggerian thought can be divorced from the phenomenon of Heidegger's prose style.

To Heidegger's detractors, this style is an abomination. It is nothing more than bombastic, indecipherable jargon. It is, furthermore, not only instrumental in Heidegger's personal engagement with Nazism but symptomatic of a general maelstrom of pseudoprofundity and archaism that infected the German language from Herder to Hitler. This is the verdict which gives animus to the dissection of Heideggerian language in T. W. Adorno's *Jargon der*

Eigentlichkeit (*The Jargon of Specificity*, 1964) and to the wicked pastiche of Heidegger's style in Günter Grass's novel *Hundejahre* (*Dog Years*, published in the same year).

On Heideggerians, in contrast, the language of the master exercises a mesmeric force. It literally spellbinds, making the prose of other philosophers and even the work of contemporary poets seem shallow. Heidegger's play on the hidden life of words, his pulsating cadence, his use of metonymy, in which concrete attributes stand for abstract entities and abstract segments represent or enact a concrete whole, seem to become simultaneously transparent and hypnotic, like a deep seen through a film of light or lit water. Sartre's principal philosophic work, *L'Etre et le néant* (*Being and Nothingness*), reflects this fascination. It seeks to translate or, rather, modulate into French the opaque strength of Heideggerian German. Currently, the French school of psychoanalysis, under Jacques Lacan, and the French school of semiotics, led by Jacques Derrida, are trying to achieve in their own tongue Heidegger's etymological immersion. The poetry of Celan is shot through with Heideggerian neologisms and word-welding.

My immediate task is not to take sides, *pro* or *contra*. The problem is more perplexing and inhibiting. It is a fact that many native speakers of German, even when they possess a fair measure of philosophic literacy, find much in Heidegger incomprehensible. They quite literally cannot make out what Heidegger is saying and whether, indeed, he is really saying anything. The attempt, as I must make it, to rephrase in English a good many of Heidegger's key notions and formulations is utterly implausible. There is evidence that Heidegger himself would have viewed it as both quixotic and undesirable. He had praise for what his translators achieved in *Being and Time*. But he regarded efforts at translating his other writings, and the later texts in particular, into any other language as largely wasted. Such was the total inherence of his meaning in German and in its linguistic past. Yet even this is not the heart of the difficulty.

I am not convinced that Martin Heidegger wanted to be "understood" in the customary sense of that word; that he wanted an understanding which would entail the possibility of restating his views by means of a more or less close paraphrase. An ancient epigram on Heraclitus, in so many respects Heidegger's model, admonishes the reader: "Do not be in too great a hurry to get to the end of Heraclitus the Ephesian's book; the path is hard to travel. Gloom is there and darkness devoid of light. But if an initiate be your guide, the path shines brighter than sunlight." Initiation is not understanding in the ordinary sense. Heidegger conceives of his ontology, of his poetics of thought, to be such that they cannot, finally, be reconciled to the manner of ratiocination and linear argument that has governed Western official consciousness after Plato. To "understand" Heidegger is to accept entry into an alternative order or space of meaning and of being. If we grasped him readily or were able to communicate his intent in other words than his own, we would already have made the leap out of Western metaphysics (I will try to clarify later what Heidegger means by this designation). We would, in a very strong sense, no longer have any need of Heidegger. It is not "understanding" that Heidegger's discourse solicits primarily. It is an "experiencing," an acceptance of felt strangeness. We are asked to suspend in ourselves the conventions of common logic and unexamined grammar in order to "hear," to "stand in the light of"—all these are radical Heideggerian notions—the nearing of elemental truths and possibilities, of apprehension long buried under the frozen crust of habitual, analytically credible saying.

Even if put in this clumsy way, Heidegger's demand seems to be a sort of mystical bullying. Yet I can testify that much of Heidegger does "get through," though in ways not readily identifiable with the usual modes of understanding and "re-statability" (already, and this is part of the dilemma, one finds oneself groping for new words). These ways compare with our gradual comprehension, or "sufferance," of great poetry; there, also, paraphrase and analytic diagnosis are often empty. And they compare, perhaps crucially, with the ways in which we grasp and make our own the meanings of music. But even if one is not deceiving oneself about such ways of reception and internalization, these will not translate into any other terms in their own language or, *a fortiori*, into those of any other tongue. To write in German about Heidegger's German is arduous enough. To do so in English, a language natively hostile to certain orders of abstruseness and metaphoric abstraction, is well-nigh impossible. Linguistic philosophy and the language of philosophy at best find themselves in a paradoxical condition: that of attempting to jump "outside" and beyond the speaker's own shadow. This vaulting is one of Heidegger's essential methods and aims (he calls it "the overcoming of metaphysics"). But like Plotinus, himself not, perhaps, in the customary sense a philosopher, Heidegger operates in the shadow-area between rational speech and "something else." It is almost a contradiction to expect daylight clarity.

Numerous adversaries, not only Theodor Adorno and Günter Grass, relate the "disaster" of Heidegger's style to that of his politics. This is our fourth crux. The dossier on Heidegger's pronouncements and activities in 1933–34 is voluminous. But despite or because of a veritable blizzard of indictments and apologias by critics and supporters, it remains extremely difficult to get at the facts. Just what, for example, was Heidegger's conduct toward his former master and patron, the "non-Aryan" Husserl? It is not clear to me, moreover, that the essential questions have been asked. What, if any, are the connections between the doctrines and idiom of *Being and Time* and those of National Socialism? And what explanation can be offered to account for Heidegger's total refusal, *after 1945*, to say anything candid or even intelligible either about his personal record under Nazism or about the general holocaust? But it may be that this is not the moment in which these two questions can be stringently formulated and pressed home. We are at once too near and too far. Nazi barbarism and its consequences continue to affect our consciousness and the landscape of reference. This afterlife is, or ought to be, so vivid as to make of dispassion an indecency. And indeed to many who have direct experience of them, the ambience, the details, the "feel" of existence and sensibility in the National Socialist era already seem remote or suppressed from exact remembrance. Thus it becomes very nearly impossible to reconstruct authoritatively the psychological intent, the material circumstances, of this or that episode in Heidegger's conduct at Freiburg during the months following Hitler's rise to power and during the war years. Yet some attempt at such reconstruction is unavoidable in even a summary portrait of the man and his works.

These objective handicaps are worrying enough. But I must add a more personal note. I am not a professional philosopher. It is not altogether obvious what is meant by this rubric, and Heidegger himself would repudiate the phrase. But we can take it as signifying someone whose discipline of activity or of teaching is recognized as professional by colleagues and students in the field, by the editors of the relevant philosophic journals, and, so far as it takes note of the question at all, by the educated community at large. Thus we know, roughly at least, what is meant by the proposition that J. L. Austin was "a professional philosopher," while Albert Camus, many of whose writings may be of overt philosophic content and interest, was not. My own field is that of the study of language, of its relations to literature on the one hand and to the history of ideas and society on the other. Two German terms, for neither of which English has an equivalent, *Sprachphilosoph* and *Kulturkritiker,* more or less cover the ground. This means that there are substantive areas in Heidegger's work, such as his interpretations of Aristotelian logic and Kantian epistemology, his early conflicts with the German neo-Kantians such as Cassirer, or the technical aspects of *Vom Wesen des Grundes,* 1929 (translated as *The Essence of Reasons* in 1969) which lie outside my real competence. Yet I must touch on them to fill in one or another part of the general picture. And because I am not a professional philosopher, whatever I can say with regard to Heidegger's stature and of the location of his work within philosophy as it is now understood and taught will be vulnerable.

Given these external pitfalls and personal inadequacies, why then try to write this essay? Again, I must answer personally. For many years, my own work has borne principally on three domains. First, there is that of the tragic reading of man and of man's relations to the state which has its dual source in Greek tragedy and in the emblematic episode of the death of Socrates. Second, there is the manifold problem of the nature and development of language and, especially, of the possibilities and constraints on translation both within and between human tongues (the mystery of imperfect or ready understanding). Third, I have sought to formulate certain questions about the interactions between, the interpenetrations of, artistic, philosophic, and scientific achievements on one hand, and the totalitarian barbarisms of the twentieth century on the other. To ask such questions is to revert, obsessively perhaps, to the relations between German culture and Nazism, an interweaving in which the German language, of which Goethe and Kant but also Hitler are master practitioners, plays a determining role.

In each of these three areas, I have found Heidegger to be massively present and in the path of further thinking. His preoccupation with the roots of Greek thought and with Sophocles' tragic vision is central. He has said things about human language as radical, as universally provocative in their implications, as any said since Plato. His gestures and silences in respect of Nazism, his literal immanence in the destiny of the German language before, during, and after the years of final inhumanity, make of Heidegger a touchstone for a "politics of the word." Thus I have found myself compelled to enter into the world of Heidegger's discourse, to try to follow the *Holzwege*, the "fire-breaks" or "lumbermen's trails," which, to use his own constant simile, may lead us toward the *Lichtung*, the "clearing" in our own existence. I have found myself attempting, often via dissent, to read Plato, Sophocles, Hölderlin—the "poet's poet," as Heidegger names him—in the light and shadow of Heidegger's commentaries. And I have come to believe that Heidegger's use and exploration of the seventeenth-century Pietist tag *Denken ist Danken*, "to think is to thank," may well be indispensable if we are to carry on as articulate and moral beings. The figure of Martin Heidegger himself makes this conviction at once more insistent and paradoxical.

These concerns determine the limits of my treatment. There is no cause for biography except at the one dark knot. Heidegger was born on September 26, 1889, in Messkirch, in the Black Forest region of Baden-Württemberg. It was in Messkirch that he died eighty-six years later. His father was sexton in the Catholic church, and Heidegger's early life was steeped in Catholicism. It was from a cleric that the teen-age boy received the book that was, very largely, to initiate and shape his own intellectual history: *Von der mannigfachen Bedeutung des Seienden nach Aristoteles* (*On the Manifold Meaning of Being According to Aristotle*) published in 1862 by the Catholic thinker Franz Brentano. Heidegger studied at Freiburg under Heinrich Rickert, a neo-Kantian, and under Husserl, the begetter of modern phenomenology. He received his doctorate in 1914, was excused from active service on grounds of health, and achieved his *Habilitation* (the degree needed to teach in a German university) with a thesis on the doctrine of categories in Duns Scotus (1916). His own activities as a lecturer had already begun in Freiburg during the winter semester of 1915. From 1920 to 1923, Heidegger was Husserl's assistant at Freiburg, a relationship that, in German academic usage, implies both a close personal and ideological affinity and the prospect of succession. After a spell at the University of Marburg (1923–28), Heidegger succeeded Husserl in the chair of philosophy at Freiburg. His inaugural lecture was the famous *Was ist Metaphysik*, first published in 1929. Heidegger taught at Freiburg until November 1944. The Allied authorities suspended him from all teaching for the period 1945–51. Professor Heidegger retired in 1959. During the later years of his academic activity, Heidegger spent more and more time at Todtnauberg, a refuge in the Black Forest whose evocative name and solitude have become synonymous with the close-guarded character of Heidegger's private life and the forest images that punctuate his writing. Heidegger traveled very rarely: to Davos in 1929 for what was to become the celebrated polemic exchange on Kant and idealism with Ernst Cassirer; two or three times to Provence where, in 1955 and again in 1968, disciples and friends such as the poet René Char and the painter Georges Braque arranged informal seminars; a late visit to Greece. Like the life of Kant, on which he may at some points have patterned his own, Heidegger's career, with its rootedness in one place, with its almost total refusal, certainly after February 1934, of external eventuality or contingency, poses and exemplifies the very rare, indeed troubling, case of a human existence invested totally in abstract thought. What is it like to live continuously in the exercise of esoteric reflection? The question ought to be borne in mind when one gauges the concreteness, the existential density that Heidegger attaches to *das Denken* and its derivatives, *das Andenken, das Durchdenken, das Bedenken* ("a thinking on and of," "a thinking through," "a thinking about, toward, on behalf of"), which crowd his vocabulary. One point is clear: in Heidegger's biography the dates that matter are those of the lectures and seminars he gave at Freiburg and at Marburg.[1] Few lives have been so uncompromisingly the husk of a teaching.

From this teaching, I propose to select a number of pivotal themes and moments. Much will be left out, including such highly significant works as the articles collected in *Identität und Differenz* (1957)[2] or the two-volume *Nietzsche* of 1961, an oddly pedestrian commentary whose more original arguments are present, and more incisively so, in other texts. Furthermore, I will touch only cursorily on the vexed issue of Heidegger's

[1] They are listed chronologically in an appendix to Fr. William J. Richardson's invaluable *Heidegger: Through Phenomenology to Thought*, 1963.
[2] Available in English as *Essays in Metaphysics: Identity and Difference*, 1960.

derivation and deviance from the orthodox phenomenology of Husserl. On this point, Husserl himself remained uncertain. And even where an essay or lecture or section of *Sein und Zeit* is looked at closely, numerous aspects will be neglected.

But this may not be as disabling as it would be in the case of other thinkers and philosophic constructs. In essence, the voluminous totality of Martin Heidegger's argument bears on one single topic: what he calls "the being of Being." The process of meditation is an inward-spiraling motion that leads, always, to this one center. As we shall see, any one of a cluster of Heideggerian pronouncements can be shown to enclose, often explicitly, and by virtue of their singular terminology, the whole of Heidegger's doctrine of existence. It may, therefore, be possible to touch on the heart of the matter even in an introductory study that does no more than ask: *How is a page of Heidegger to be read, what orders of meaning can be drawn from it?* Heidegger himself insists that it is only the right asking which matters. He says, in what becomes a litany, that it is never the goal which counts, but only the journey, and even the first small step on the journey. Many of his titles are those of peregrination: *Holzwege, Wegmarken, Unterwegs zur Sprache, Der Feldweg* ("the fire-break," "road markers," "on the way toward speech," "the path across the field"). He has been an indefatigable walker in unlit places. Let us see how far we can follow, or wish to do so.

Some Basic Terms

i

"*Was ist das—die Philosophie?*" asked Heidegger
at a colloquium held in France in August 1955.[1]
The interrogative start is, of course, traditional
in philosophic exposition and points back to the
Socratic dialectic. But Heidegger's title does not
read "*What Is Philosophy?*" as in the translation.
Its actual phrasing is deliberately helpless and
halting. It suggests a two-part question. The stress
lies as heavy on *ist* and on *das* as it does on
Philosophie. Before naming the object of inquiry
("philosophy"), Heidegger makes salient and
problematic the processes of predication and ob-
jectivization. He intimates (and this intimation

[1] The English-language version of his lecture, by W.
Kluback and J. T. Wilde (1958), was published bilin-
gually. This ought to be the case with all of Heidegger's writings, as recourse to the special terminology
and grammatical structure of the original is virtually
indispensable.

19

is at once the source and core of his entire thought) that *ist,* the postulate of existence, is previous to and crucial within any meaningful question; and he suggests that *das,* the *quid est*—the "quiddity" as the schoolmen would say—the "whatness" to which this or indeed any serious question addresses itself is a profoundly complex postulate. Such a postulate of integral presence may be unavoidable, but it is not to be invoked unexamined. Furthermore, by setting off *die Philosophie,* by compelling a hiatus and pause between the most general form of ontological query (namely, "What *is* this or that or anything?") and the object actually in view, Heidegger achieves a subtle twofold effect. He makes the notion "philosophy," of which we might have claimed an everyday, confident control, somewhat strange and distant; and he makes it dependent on, ancillary to, the greater, more pressing question and notion of "isness" and "whatness." Thus a fuller translation of his title could read: "What is it to ask—what this thing, philosophy, *is?*"

It is our task, begins Heidegger, to set discussion on its way, to bring it "onto a path." The indefinite article is intended to underline the postulate that this path is only one among many, and that there is no a priori guarantee that it will conduct us to our goal. It is Heidegger's constant strategy to show that the process of undertaking, the motion on the way, not only precedes the attainment of whatever goal we have set ourselves yet, as we shall see, in some sense equals this goal in dignity and meaning. But although the path chosen will be one of many, it must lie inside the forest. It must give us the assurance "that we are moving within philosophy and not outside of it and around it." This qualification is consequential: it implies the famous dilemma of the "hermeneutic circle": we attempt to define a thing by the use of attributes that already presume a definition. It implies that there are other paths which lead *out* of the forest and thus *mis*lead (e.g., the history of philosophy, the analysis of philosophic arguments as being the ideological manifest of socioeconomic forces, the view of philosophy as an allegoric preface to the exact sciences, and so on). A path, says Heidegger, not *any* path.

The customary paths are those which begin with a definition, even if and especially where this definition is subsequently to be dismissed or radically refined (as in the Socratic method). Heidegger offers: philosophy not only is something rational but "is the actual guardian of reason." For "reason" he does not use *Vernunft*, but *ratio*, the Latin term with its Aristotelian overtones. "Guardian" is *Verwalterin*, a word that includes resonances, crucial for Heidegger, of "trusteeship," the active "custodianship" of inherited substance. Even cursory reflection, however, shows that this path will lead nowhere. By introducing the concept of "reason" or "rationality," we have merely substituted one unknown for another. The Heideggerian *Weg*, the woodsman's trail, is quite different. "And only because it is the nearest at hand is it difficult to find." (Heidegger treasures, and reverts insatiably to, this paradox of proximity, this finding, which is both Socratic and phenomenological, that the highest densities of meaning lie in the immediate, in the most obviously "at hand.") We are asking: "What *is* this whatness—which we name philosophy?" We are asking a *word* to disclose itself. How can there be disclosure if we do not listen closely, if we seek to press up on the object of our inquiry some previous or ready-made analytic formula? If we hear "the word 'philosophy' coming to us from its source, it sounds thus: *philosophia*. Now the word 'philosophy' is speaking Greek. The word, as a Greek word, is a path."

Here we have before us *the* most characteristic and disputed move in Heidegger's method: the argument from and through etymology. The manifold uses of this argument, and Heidegger's justification of it, will preoccupy us throughout this book. What needs emphasis at this preliminary point is the full generative and evidential aim of Heidegger's maneuver. *"Das Wort 'Philosophie' spricht jetzt griechisch."* This means, literally, that the *word itself*, if we hear it rightly, *speaks Greek*. It is not *we* who are using a word that happens to be derived from the classical Greek lexicon. The power and agency of statement lie *inside* the word *philosophia* (which Heidegger does not transcribe, but sets on the page in its Greek characters). It is *language that speaks*, not, or not primordially, man. This, again, is a cardinal Heideggerian postulate, to which I must return. And what does the word tell us? "The word *philosophia* tells us that philosophy is something that, first of all, determines the existence of the Greek world. Not only that—*philosophia* also determines the innermost basic feature of our Western-European history." ("Innermost basic feature" is an honest attempt at rendering *Grundzug*. In German, and most notably in Heideggerian German, *Grund* portends intensely concrete but also numinous strains of rootedness, of earthly ancientness and provenance.) *Philosophia* is, therefore, the foundation and shaping impetus of Western history. And because it is Greek in its nature and in the articulation that alone can give it authentic meaning and continued existence, philosophy demands of those who would apprehend it, of those whose "path of asking" is truly inward and disinterested, that they rethink the full range of its implications as these were experienced and voiced by the Greeks. (I am, at this stage, leaving to one side the obvious challenge as to whether any such rethinking is possible, as to whether meditation on etymology, however probing, can go upstream in time and discover primal sources. What we want to do initially is to see how Heidegger conducts his argument.)

It is not only "philosophy" that is Greek: it is "also *how* we question, the manner in which, even today, we ask the question." For to ask What is that? is to ask *ti estin?* an interrogation whose terms are the seed and dynamic articulation of Greek (therefore of all subsequent Western) thought. The meanings assigned to "what" will vary as between Plato and Aristotle or as between Kant and Hegel. The Platonic Idea is not the Aristotelian "substance" or the Kantian "thing in itself." But the underlying question and the verbal form of the question—the two being for Heidegger wholly fused—are Greek. In asking about isness and whatness, in referring this asking to "philosophy," "we are peculiarly summoned back" to the Greek wellspring. We are "reclaimed for and by it as soon as we not only utter the words of the question 'What is philosophy?' but reflect upon its meaning." In German, "origin," "source" can be *Herkunft*—literally the place from which we came, the "provenance of our coming." Heidegger's *zurückgerufen* and *re-klamiert* carry an almost physical edge. There is a "re-vocation," a "summoning back to" the place of our inception and instauration. It is that of Greek speech and thought or, more exactly, "speech-thought." Nor is it any question that we are asking, that we are being "revoked by": "it is *the* question of our Western-European actuality and being," our *Dasein*, which, as we shall see, is Heidegger's primary term. If, therefore,

we enter into the total and original meaning of the question "What is philosophy?" then our question has, through its historical origin, found a direction into the historical future. We have found a path. The question itself is a path. It leads from the actual being of the Greek world [*von dem Dasein des Griechentums*] down to us, if not, indeed, beyond us. We are—if we persist in this question—traveling on a clearly indicated path.

Where does it lead?

At first, it would appear, to mere circularity. Questions, and this too is a Heideggerian postulate, are only worth asking of that which is worth questioning, of that "which is questionable in a sense implying not the guarantee of an answer, but at least that of an informing response." But in order to know whether philosophy "has become worthy of question," we must know beforehand, to a greater or lesser degree, what philosophy *is* (a familiar Socratic ambush). Heidegger does not fear this hermeneutic circularity. If we treat it stringently, it can become an inward-guiding spiral. Once more, the key is language:

> If we listen now and later to the words of the Greek language, then we move into a distinct and distinguished domain. Slowly it will dawn upon our thinking that the Greek language is no mere language like the European languages known to us. The Greek language, and it alone, is *logos*. . . . In the Greek language what is said *is* at the same time, and in an eminent way, that which it is called (designated as). If we hear a Greek word with a Greek ear, we follow its *legein* (its speaking), its direct, immediate presentation of what it says. What it presents is that which lies immediately before us. Through the audible Greek word we are directly in the presence of the thing itself, not first in the presence of a mere word-sign.

In what way this assertion does no more than reproduce the allegories of Adamic speech and of Hebrew as we find them in Cabalistic and Pietist doctrines, and what conceivable means there could be of verifying Heidegger's claims, are legitimate and, indeed, urgent questions. What we want to know now, however, is just where this "etymologizing realism" is taking us.

The answer is: to yet further etymologies, which Heidegger's critics hold to be wildly arbitrary. (Even if this is what they should ultimately prove to be, it is worth stressing that they emerge from the cumulative impetus of Heidegger's previous writings, that the Heideggerian lexicon is, with certain exceptions, internally consistent.) The word *philosophos* "was presumably coined by Heraclitus," for whom there was as yet no such thing as "philosophy." It signified "one who loves the *sophon.*" But in this context, specifies Heidegger, *philein*, "to love," has that particular Heraclitean sense which we find also in *homologein: "so sprechen wie der Lógos spricht, d.h. dem Lógos entsprechen."* We must try to translate this "translation": "to speak as the Logos speaks, which is itself the living core, the 'is' of speech; to correspond to the Logos by responding to it, by being its echo and true counterstatement" (all of these figures of reciprocity being active in the prefix *en-* in *entsprechen*). "That one being reciprocally unites itself with another, that both are originally united with each other because they are at each other's disposal [*zueinander verfügt sind*]—this *harmonia* is the distinctive feature of *philein*, of 'loving' in the Heraclitean sense." And what of *sophon*? According to Heraclitus's own conception, says Heidegger, *sophon* aims at, makes manifest, the insight that "One is all" (*Panta ta onta*). This insight is founded on and makes sovereignly explicit the fact that "all being is in Being. To put it more pointedly, being *is* Being." The translation here is straightforward, but the proposition is so central that it should be set out in its original: *"Alles Seiende ist im Sein; das Sein ist das Seiende."*

Even someone acquainted with Heidegger only summarily or via a notice in a general encyclopedia will know that these two affirmations, which are in fact identical and indivisible, constitute the essence of Heidegger's

teaching. *Das Seiende,* being, and *das Sein,* Being, are
the exclusive, unwavering object of Martin Heidegger's
lifelong meditation and discourse. What it is that they
"mean" (leaving aside, for now, the crucial question as to
whether "meaning" is the category most suitable to their
spirit and function); why it is that we use a lower case
for our translation of *das Seiende* and capitalize the one
for *das Sein,* thus contrasting "being," the extant, with
"Being," the "isness" of existence; can any other concept
or set of terms stand in their place? These are the questions, this is the *one* question, to which every reader of
Heidegger must address himself. I hope to do so step by
step. All we know now is that the inquiry *Was ist das—
die Philosophie?* and Heidegger's insistence that the problem inheres in our understanding of certain Greek words
and turns of thought have brought us to the absolute
heart of the Heideggerian world.

Even before the path has properly begun to reveal itself to us, we have been thrust to the center. We stand at
the *Lichtung,* or clearing, in the innermost part of the
forest. Has this happened because we are looking at a
summarizing lecture from Heidegger's later period? This
might account for the peremptory directness of argument
and definition, but not for the substance of the argument
itself. "Being" and "being" are the pivot, the core of "lit
darkness" to which every path leads, whatever its starting point on the wide circumference of Heidegger's work.

Heidegger goes on: "All being is in Being. To hear such
a thing sounds trivial to our ear, if not, indeed, offensive,
for no one needs to bother about the fact that being belongs to Being. All the world knows that being is that
which is. What else remains for being but to be? And yet,
just this fact that being is gathered together in Being,
that in the appearance of Being being appears, astonished
the Greeks and first astonished them and them alone."

These sentences crystallize Heidegger's doctrine of existence and his methodological stance, which is one of radical astonishment. The fact of existence, of being in Being, astonishes Heidegger immeasurably. These sentences also lead toward what it is that philosophy does: "Philosophy seeks what being is insofar as it is. Philosophy is *en route* to the Being of beings, that is, to being with respect to Being."

Let me attempt a crude, preliminary restatement or circumspection. It is the unique and specific business of philosophy, therein and at all times referential to its Greek inception, to be incessantly astonished at and focused on the fact that all things *are;* that there is a universal and totally determinant attribute to things, which is that of existence. This astonishment and the meditation it entails—what Heidegger will call "the thinking of Being," "the endeavor to think Being"—sets philosophy on the way toward the question of what *it* is that *is*, of what it is that indwells in all extant things, of what it is that constitutes beingness (as opposed, in the first and obvious alternative, to "non-being" or to such existential particulars as "redness," "largeness," "function," and so on).

Socrates and Plato were the first to take "the steps into philosophy." This is to say, they were the first to pose the question of existence in an analytic-rational guise. Theirs is a great achievement, says Heidegger, but (and here he is following a Nietzschean paradox) also a symptom of decline. Anaximander, Heraclitus, and Parmenides, who came before, did not need to be "philosophers." They were "thinkers" (*Denker*), men caught in the radical astonishment (*Thaumazein*) of being. They belonged to a primal, therefore "more authentic" dimension or experience of thinking, in which beingness was immediately present to language, to the *logos*. Just what it signifies to experience and to speak being in this primary and "thoughtful" way is something that Heidegger labors to explain, to illustrate, and, above all, to "act out" in his late writings.

For Plato the Being of beings resides in eternal, immutable matrices of perfect form, or "Ideas," for Aristotle in what he calls the *energeia,* the unfolding actuality that realizes itself in substance. The Platonic notion engenders the whole of Western metaphysics down to the time of Nietzsche. The Aristotelian concept, with its concomitant investigation into "first causes" and "dynamic principles," lays the foundations of our science and technology.

For Heidegger, neither of these two legacies, the idealist-metaphysical and/or the scientific-technological, satisfies the original, authentic condition and task of thought which is to experience, to think through the nature of existence, the "Beingness of being." From *Sein und Zeit* onward, Heidegger conceives it as his essential enterprise to "overthrow" (in a sense yet to be defined) the metaphysical and scientific traditions that have governed Western argument and history since Plato and Aristotle. Heidegger will urge relentlessly that these two great currents of idealization and analysis have sprung not from a genuine perception of Being but from a *forgetting of Being,* from a taking-for-granted of the central existential mystery. More than this: Heidegger will seek to prove that it is the continued authority of the metaphysical-scientific way of looking at the world, a way almost definitional of the West, that has brought on, has, in fact, made unavoidable the alienated, unhoused, recurrently barbaric estate of modern technological and mass-consumption man. "After two and a half thousand years it would seem to be about time to see being in respect of *what* it *is* insofar as it is being [*im Hinblick darauf, was*

es ist, insofern es Seiendes ist]." It is precisely this vision
that has been dimmed or forgotten outright since philosophy, in the Socratic sense, began.

Having said this, Heidegger performs a characteristic
move. He begins all over again. To ask in "philosophic"
terms—i.e., in Platonic, Aristotelian, or Kantian terms—
"What is this thing—philosophy?" is to guarantee a
"philosophic" answer. It is to remain trapped in the circle
of the dominant Western tradition, and *this* circle, in contrast to what Heidegger takes to be inward-circling paths
of thinking, is sterile. We must, therefore, attempt a different sort of discourse, another kind of asking. The
crucial motion turns on the meaning of *Ent-sprechen.* An
Ent-sprechen is not "an answer to" (*une réponse à*), but
a "response to," a "correspondence with," a dynamic reciprocity and matching such as occur when gears, both
in quick motion, mesh. Thus, our question as to the
nature of philosophy calls not for an answer in the sense
of a textbook definition or formulation, be it Platonic,
Cartesian, or Lockeian, but for an *Ent-sprechung,* a response, a vital echo, a "re-sponsion" in the liturgical sense
of participatory engagement. And this response or correspondence will *answer to* the being of Being. (Note that
the English phrase "to answer to" has precisely the weight
that Heidegger would ascribe to it, signifying as it does
both "response" and "responsibility." A "thinker," as distinct from a post-Socratic or academic philosopher, is
"answerable to" the question of being.)

This "answering to" comes to pass through a dialogue
with "that which has been handed down to us as the Being of being." But such a dialogue cannot derive from or
within the history of philosophy as it is commonly practiced. This is one of Heidegger's characteristic injunc-
tions. It is not by making and transmitting summaries of
what Aristotle, or Hume, or Fichte have said that we

consciousness are *not* the center, the assessors of existence. Man is only a privileged listener and respondent to existence. The vital relation to otherness is not, as for Cartesian and positivist rationalism, one of "grasping" and pragmatic use. It is a relation of audition. We are trying "to listen to the voice of Being." It is, or ought to be, a relation of extreme responsibility, custodianship, answerability to and for. Of this answerability, the thinker and the poet, *der Denker und der Dichter*, are at once the carriers and the trustees. This is because it is in their oneness to language (to the *logos*), in their capacity to *be spoken* rather to speak—a distinction that will become more intelligible as we proceed—that the truth, or can we say with Wordsworth and Hölderlin "the music of being," most urgently calls for and summons up response.

Hence the final attempt (which is, in fact, the fifth) at definition in this 1955 lecture. Philosophy is a "distinctive manner of language," a manner that interconnects thought with poetry because "in the service of language both intercede on behalf of language and give lavishly of themselves." (*Verwenden und verschwenden* is more expressive, meaning both a "turning inward from" and "waste" of self.) If philosophy, therefore, is truly a co-respondence that makes articulate, that renders audible and is answerable to the summons (*der Zuspruch*) of the Being of being, it is to the "thinkers" we must turn, not to the metaphysicians and pragmatic knowers. It is in the veiled force of original meaning in Greek words that we may find *philosophia*, in certain elements of Oriental meditation (there is, in the later Heidegger, an encounter with Japanese ascetic speculation), and above all in the elect poets: Hölderlin, Rilke, George, Trakl. Coleridge would have recognized precisely what Heidegger is after. As he put it: "in Wonder all Philosophy began." (And it is only to recognize the idiosyncrasy, the tangled roots of

Heidegger's position to recall that this dictum is, itself, taken from Plato.)

Already it is plain that we shall get nowhere in our attempt to learn how to read a page of Heidegger, and in our attempt to find out whether the result justifies the labor, if we do not come to grips with the two cardinal terms "Being" (*das Sein*) and "being" (*das Seiende*). In one sense, we would find ourselves engaging these two terms at any and every point in Heidegger's writings. In another, however, we can see that they form the specific core of several interrelated texts. These include *Was ist Metaphysik?* (1929); the 1943 afterword to the fourth edition (1943); the introduction appended to the fifth edition (1949); the *Brief über den Humanismus* (*Letter on "Humanism"*), which Heidegger addressed to his French disciple Jean Beaufret in the autumn of 1946, and which was published the following year; the *Einführung in die Metaphysik*, which dates back to 1935 but was published only in 1953; *Zur Seinsfrage* (literally *On the Beingquestion*), Heidegger's contribution of 1955 to the sixtieth-birthday commemoration of his friend and political counterpart, the novelist and publicist Ernst Jünger.[2]

All these texts presume *Sein und Zeit*, which had, of course, appeared in 1927. I am, as it were, trying to proceed upstream. But this, as we have noted, is precisely Heidegger's own tactic. By mapping something of the complex life of "beingness" in these subsequent treatments, I hope to make both clearer and more necessary the nature of their source in Heidegger's first *summa*. But there is a second difficulty. It is in the writings that I shall

---

[2] *The Question of Being*, translated by Kluback and Wilde, 1959; and the text of the four seminars on the sum of his teaching which Heidegger conducted in France between September 1966 and September 1973.

now draw on that Heideggerian specialists locate the *Kehre,* the possible turn of language and meaning from the earlier to the later teachings. Heidegger himself insists on the organic continuity of the ontological concept throughout his whole work (even where *Sein* becomes the archaic, eccentric *Seyn*). The successive addenda to the 1929 inaugural lecture constitute an exercise in both continuity and modulation. They enact thought in progress. Moreover, there is the constant paradigm of circularity, of the forest-ways radiating from and arrowing toward an unwavering center. Insofar as it "thinks" and "thinks on" Being, each of the texts I cite is inwoven in that reticulation of which *Sein und Zeit* is at once the animating source and the center.

Heidegger was fortunate. *His* question—the one and total question that quickened his life into thought—appears to have overwhelmed him early, most probably in his late teens. I have referred to the impact on Heidegger of Brentano's study of the manifold senses of being according to Aristotle, which he read in the summer of 1907. There may have been other instigations also: the relaxation of a strict Catholicism into a secular, yet patently related, sense and vocabulary of the absolute; an almost uncanny personal sensibility to the grain and substance of physical existence, to the "thingness" and obstinate quiddity of things, be they rock or tree or human presence. Like Gerard Manley Hopkins, who was also steeped in Scholastic attempts to delineate the exact mystery of substance and who was also overwhelmed by the radiant autonomy of organic and inorganic objects, Heidegger felt the world with a rare concreteness.

But whatever its didactic or psychological sources, the one wonder that was to preside over Heidegger's life declared itself early and inescapably: *Why are there essents, existents, things that are, rather than nothing?* Leibniz had put it this way: *Pourquoi il y a plutôt quelque chose que rien?* Heidegger was to rephrase the question in a number of ways, notably: "What is the Being [*das Sein*] which renders possible all being [*das Seiende*]?" But it is always the same question: Why *is* there anything or something or everything, when there could *be nothing* (and, as we shall see, this latter alternative of existential nullity is not for Heidegger a mere void or grammatical fiction)? In short, Heidegger is a man literally overcome by the notion of "is" (Greek *on*), a man inexhaustibly astonished by the fact of existence, and haunted by the reality of that *other* possibility, which is nothingness (Sartre's *néant*).

For the great majority of human beings, this question of being looms "in moments of great despair, when things tend to lose all their weight and all meaning becomes obscured." Or it can be experienced in flashes of vital brilliance, when sensory discrimination pierces the skin of things. But in most cases, this question "will strike but once like a muffled bell that rings into our life and gradually dies away." For Heidegger, however, it is the one and only interrogation, the incessant asking without which there can be neither a proper humanity, nor a coherent mode of individual and social existence, nor any philosophy worthy of the name. Let us be quite certain that we understand just what it is that is being asked.

The question does not concern itself with any particular essent: "An elephant in an Indian jungle 'is' just as much as some chemical combustion process at work on the planet Mars." Chalk *is* and so is cheese. The question Heidegger is asking keeps its distance from every particular and individual object, phenomenon, presence, from every this and that. To ask *why* there is being instead of nothingness is to ask of the foundations (*Ursprung, Urgrund*) of all things. But it is also, and explicitly, to put in ques-

tion the nature of the questioner himself (this will lead
to the Heideggerian notion of *Dasein*, of that in man
which "is there"), and it comports a constant questioning
of the language which enables us to, or inhibits us from,
posing the question in the first place. Thus the world, the
human questions, and the speech in which he questions
are the triple constant in Heidegger's ceaseless, circling,
inward-driving query: "Why is there? Why is there not
nothing?"

This question, insists Heidegger, is not theological.
Whether the account of creation in the Bible or in any
other religious system be true or false is immaterial. It
can supply no answer to the question of being as Heidegger conceives it. "To philosophize is to ask: 'Why are
there essents rather than nothing?'" From the point of
view of faith, such a question is folly, but "philosophy is
this very foolishness." (Note how Heidegger inverts the
scriptural and Kierkegaardian notion of the "foolishness"
of the questions posed by Christ.) To ask as does Heidegger is "a daring attempt to fathom this unfathomable . . .
to push our questioning to the very end. Where such an
attempt occurs there is philosophy." As we saw, Heidegger
means something radically different from Platonic, Cartesian, or Kantian metaphysical inquiries. The claim put
forward is immense and troubling. Philosophy, in the
Heideggerian sense, "is a thinking that breaks the paths
for, that opens the perspective of, that kind of knowing
which sets the norms and values of the knowledge in and
through which a people fulfills itself historically and
culturally. The knowledge that comes of such thinking
kindles and necessitates all inquiries, and thereby threatens all values." The closing phrase is, of course, Nietzschean; and the national, collective overtones are to be
borne in mind. Furthermore, it is the very nature and task
of the "beingquestion," which constitutes *philosophia*,

"never to make things easier, but only more difficult."
Hence the language problem.

Heidegger is well aware that the question he is asking,
and the discourse that arises from this asking, will use a
language that

> strikes the everyday understanding as strange, if not
> insane. How, except in a language almost insane, can
> one question the Being of being [*das Sein des Seien-
> den*], and urge that the two concepts must be kept
> apart? Nor can language, such is its strangeness and
> its strength, ever be divorced, even by a hair's breadth,
> from the questioner and his questioning. Words and
> language are not wrappings in which things are packed
> for the commerce of those who write and speak. It is
> in words and language that things first come into be-
> ing and are.

To predicate existence, to say that a thing *is,* is to speak
the being of the thing as only language can speak it, and
must. (What would be left to language if it could not
articulate existence?) Yet the situation is one of profound paradox.

In every sentence we utter, being is stated. But we do
not stop to ask ourselves what *it is* that we *are* saying or,
more exactly, what it is that allows, indeed compels us
to say *what is.* We inquire neither as to the existential
foundations of our own existence or nonexistence—the
two are formally and substantively inseparable—nor as
to the status of beingness attributed to (conferred on?)
the world by all and anything we say. It is just because
we make no such inquiry that Heidegger's question, and
the ensuing discourse, will seem to us as either "mad"
(his own word) or empty. This piece of chalk is white; it
is of such and such a chemical composition and molecular
arrangement; its elements possess this or that atomic
weight; it can be used to make visible marks on these
materials and not on others; it can be transformed by

dilution, by heat, or by cold into the following substances; and so on. What more is there to say?

Everything, proposes Heidegger. Why *is* this piece of chalk? Why *is* it when it could not be? And already we pause at the strangeness, at the seeming vacuity of the formulation. Moreover, what possible answer can there be to such a question other than tautology? The piece of chalk is because it *is* ("I am that which I am," sayeth God in tautological self-definition). But if this is indeed so, then the word "is" and the being that it predicates would be "no more than an empty word. It means nothing real, tangible, material. Its meaning is an unreal vapor. . . . Who would want to chase after such a vapor?" Make "is" into a hypostatized mystery, obscure its everyday function as a grammatical copula and you will, most assuredly, be chasing after vapors. Such is the riposte of common sense, of positivism, of the logician and the linguistic philosopher. Heidegger is entirely aware of this riposte; he invites it.

Unrepentant, he makes of this awareness the starting point of three further questions. He asks, first: How did it come about that the most important, fundamental, all-determining of concepts, that of being, should have been so drastically eroded? What "forgetting of being" has reduced our perception of "is" to that of an inert piece of syntax or a vapor? Heidegger's whole "overthrow of metaphysics," his critique of Plato, Aristotle, Leibniz, Kant, Hegel, and Nietzsche, constitutes an attempt to answer this question. To Heidegger, the history of Western civilization, seen from the two crucial vantage points of metaphysics after Plato, and of science and technology after Aristotle and Descartes, is no more and no less than the story of how being came to be forgotten. The twentieth century is the culminating but perfectly logical product of this amnesia.

This is the situation aimed at in Heidegger's second question: In what precise psychological and material ways does the condition of modern Western man, and of urban man especially, represent or act out the forgetting of being? What manner of life do we lead in a landscape of reality from which a central awareness of and reflection on the enigma of existentiality, of the presentness of essents, has all but disappeared? The attempt to give a thorough answer will inspire Heidegger's numerous discussions of technology, of the current crises of alienation and dehumanization, of that pervasive phenomenon which he calls "nihilism." When he says that Western history may well turn on the translation (the right apprehension) of the verb "to be" in a pre-Socratic fragment, Heidegger is being deadly serious. And it is this seriousness that lies at the base of his fundamentalist and apocalyptic politics.

His third question follows naturally: Has beingness passed totally from human reach, or are there processes and embodiments of experience in which the primal sense of essence remains vital and, therefore, recapturable? Is there anything left on which late-twentieth-century man can build if he is to seek a homecoming to "the house of being"? From this third question will spring Heidegger's writings on the pre-Socratics (with whom all "return" must start), on poetry, on the fine arts, and on architecture. It is this question that generates the notion of "poeticizing thought" (*das dichtende Denken*) and the fourfold construct—"gods," "heaven," "earth," and "mortals"—of the late texts. How was being forgotten; what has come of this forgetting; where and through what means can man regain remembrance? These three questions, which are really one, preoccupied and organized Heidegger's teachings and philosophical-political attitudes from the late 1920s until his death.

But it is not these three dependent, albeit vast, questions which concern us now. It is the interrogation from which they come: the "beingquestion," the *Seinsfrage* itself. As we said, this question is reiterated at every point in Heidegger's writings, often hypnotically. But sometimes, as in the *Introduction to Metaphysics*, Heidegger asks with a kind of nudging, shrewd familiarity: *Wie steht es mit dem Sein?* ("How is it with being?" "What shape is being in during these difficult days?"). This is precisely the same question as "Why are there essents rather than nothing?" but put in a preliminary, less "philosophic" way. Heidegger knows that "we are asking about something which we barely grasp, which is scarcely more than the sound of a word for us, and which puts us in danger of serving a mere word-idol when we proceed with our questioning" (a quote surely worth pondering; at his, admittedly infrequent, best as a self-critic, Heidegger more than anticipates the objections of his detractors). To help us to grasp the "barely graspable," he proceeds to examples. This move, so characteristic of most philosophic argument, is rare in Heidegger. He would have us "think being" neither by analogy nor figurative substitution but by an undeflected effort of mental and indeed physical penetration. Here is how he puts it:

We look at a building across the street. We make inventory of its dimensions, structural features, contents. Everywhere we find essents, but where, asks Heidegger, is its being? "For after all it *is*. The building *is*. If anything belongs to this essent, it is its being; yet we do not find the being inside it." Empiricists and positivists would say that Heidegger is asking a perfectly vacuous question, and that he has *verbally* postulated "being" without giving evidence that such a postulate can have any verifiable content. Heidegger would riposte: "You do exactly the same thing every time you use the word *is*, i.e., every time you utter a normal proposition. The difference is that I believe that in so doing I *am* saying something real, and am trying to find out what *it is*." Idealists would argue that the surest demonstrable existence of the building lies in the very fact that we look at it, in the process of our perception, whether this process be formative, reflexive, or some dynamic and compositional aggregate of the two. Heidegger is not prepared to allow this. Shrewdly, he invokes brute common sense: "The building stands there even if we do not look at it. We can find it only because it already *is*." He will agree with the idealist, post-Kantian constructivism and with psychological relativism that the building "alters" according to individual vision, social points of view, angles of interest, and historical convention. Such changes in phenomenological assessment are examined in depth in *Sein und Zeit*. But he insists that the "thereness" of the building, the primal fact of its existence, wholly antecedes any particular or general act of cognition (there is "recognition" precisely because the essent is there in the first place). He adds a suggestive remark: "You can, as it were, smell the being of this building in your nostrils. The smell communicates the being of this essent far more immediately and truly than any description or inspection could ever do."

Indeed, the senses are crucial to this "presence of being," to our apprehension of an *is* in things that no analytic dissection or verbal account can isolate. Heidegger's examples are at once banal and consequential. We "hear" a bird flying though, strictly speaking, the flight is not "audible"; our touch distinguishes immediately between velvet and silk, but "wherein consists the difference of their being?" A storm *is* approaching; there *was* a storm an hour ago. What do we mean by, where do we locate, its being? A distant mountain range under a broad sky *is*. Does it disclose its being to the traveler who savors the landscape, to the distant meteorologist preparing his weather map, to the farmer who makes his living in its shadow? "To all and to none," replies Heidegger. It may well be that each of these viewers is perceiving one aspect of the mountain range. But the sum of these aspects cannot be said to constitute the being of the object. This being is felt to lie "behind" or "within" the complex of aspects. What, then, *is* it? Or to cite an example that has long plagued political philosophers and those concerned with the semantics of law: a nation *is*. But where is its being situated? Not, assuredly, in the numerical collective of its inhabitants, nor in its heraldic symbols, nor, except by evasive metaphor, in the fiction of remembrance called "history." Is it, asks Heidegger, situated anywhere at all? (The strong implication is that it must be, if only because we all know the question to be meaningful.)

The next example is among Heidegger's touchstones:

A painting by van Gogh. A pair of rough peasant shoes, nothing else. Actually the painting represents nothing. But as to what *is* in that picture, you are immediately alone with it as though you yourself were making your way wearily homeward with your hoe on an evening in late fall after the last potato fires have died down. What *is* here? The canvas? The brushstrokes? The spots of color?

All of these things, which we so confidently name, are there. But the existential presentness of the painting, that in its existence which reaches into *our* being, cannot be adequately defined as the material assemblage of linseed oil, pigment, and stretched canvas. We feel, we *know*, urges Heidegger, that there *is* something else *there*, something utterly decisive. But when we seek to articulate it, "it is always as though we were reaching into the void."

We are at the heart of the argument. Let me attempt a further illustration though, damagingly I think, Heidegger continually passes it by.

To the majority of human beings, music brings moments of experience as complete, as penetrating as any they can register. In such moments, immediacy, recollection, anticipation are often inextricably fused. Music "enters" body and mind at manifold and simultaneous levels to which classifications such as "nervous," "cerebral," "somatic" apply in a rough and ready way. Music can sound in dreams. It can recede from accurate recall but leave behind an intricate ghostliness, a tension and felt lineament of motion that resemble, more or less precisely, the departed chord or harmony or relations of pitch. No less forcefully than narcotics, music can affect our mental and physical status, the minutely meshed strands of mood and bodily stance that, at any given point, define identity. Music can brace or make drowsy; it can incite or calm. It can move to tears or, mysteriously, spark laughter or, more mysteriously still, cause us to smile in what would seem to be a singular lightness, a mercurial mirth of mind as centrally rooted in us as is thought itself. We have known since Pythagoras that music can heal and since Plato that there are in music agencies that can literally madden. Melody, writes Lévi-Strauss, is the *mystère suprème* of man's humanity. But what *is* it?

Is melody the being of music, or pitch, or timbre, or the dynamic relations between tone and interval? Can we say that the being of music consists of the vibrations transmitted from the quivering string or reed to the tympanum of the ear? Is its existence to be found in the notes on the page, even if these are never sounded (what conceivable ontological status have Keats's "unheard melodies")? Modern acoustical science and electronic synthesizers are capable of breaking down analytically and then reproducing any tone or tone-combination with total precision. Does such analysis and reproduction equate with, let alone exhaust, the being of music? Where, in the phenomenon "music," do we locate the energies which can transmute the fabric of human consciousness in listener and performer?

The answer eludes us. Ordinarily, we search for metaphoric description. Wherever possible we consign the question either to technicality or to the limbo of obviousness. Yet we *know* what music *is*. We know it in the mind's echoing maze and in the marrow of our bones. We are aware of its history. We assign to it an immensity of *meaning*. This is absolutely key. Music *means*, even where, most especially where, there is no way whatever to paraphrase this meaning, to restate it in any alternative way, to set it down lexically or formally. "What, then, is music?" asks the fictive questioner from another planet. We would sing a tune or strum a piece and say, unhesitatingly, "This is music." If he asked next, "What does it mean?" the answer would be *there*, overwhelmingly, in us, but exceedingly difficult to articulate externally. Asked just this question of one of his compositions, Schumann played it again. In music, being and meaning are inextricable. They deny paraphrase. But they *are*, and our experience of this "essentiality" is as certain as any in human awareness.

Halting as it is, this analogy may suggest a first approximation to Heidegger's concept of being. Here too there is brazen obviousness and impalpability, an enveloping nearness and infinite regress. Being, in the Heideggerian sense, has, like music, a history and a meaning, a dependence on man and dimensions transcending humanity. In music, intervals are charged with sense. This, as we shall see, may help us to understand Heidegger's relation to being of an active "nothingness" (*das nicht-ende Nichts*, Sartre's *le néant*). We take the being of music for granted as we do that of the being of being. We forget to be astonished.

This forgetting, says Heidegger, is now entrenched in language. If the "question of being," the *Seinsfrage*, strikes us as vacuous, or as a mystical word game, or as purely and simply nonsense—and Heidegger knows that it is one or a combination of these reactions that make up "common sense"—the reason is, literally, linguistic. "Many words, and precisely the essential ones, are in the same situation: the language in general is worn out and used up—an indispensable but masterless means of communication that may be used as one pleases, as indifferent as a means of public transport." But the current emptiness of the word "being," the disappearance of its original strength of calling and presentness, is far more than a symptom of a general exhaustion of language. For this exhaustion is itself symptomatic of the fact that our relations to existence, which constitute the core and rationale of human speech, have receded into grammatical banality (the word "is" diminished to a mere copula) or into forgetting. Thus it follows for Heidegger that any serious inquiry into being, failing which there can be no authentic personal or public destiny, must take linguistic considerations as its starting point. Radical insight goes to the root of words.

It is hardly an exaggeration to suggest that Heideggerian thought, the ontology or "thinking of being" which Heidegger developed over some sixty-five years, derives from a grammatical feature present in German and most Western tongues but not, as it happens, in English. In German the noun "being" is *Sein* and the verb "to be" is *sein*. As in French, *être* and *être*, the noun is identical with the infinitive of the verb. In English, it is identical with a participial form. In other words, *Sein*, the verbal noun for "being," is at its syntactic base a process, an activity, a "being-there." The noun is, as it were, the momentary pause or fiction of an act; it has the same linguistic form as the act because the latter is wholly operative within it. This dynamic nominalism is fundamental to Heidegger's existential phenomenology and theory of language. But it is not with the German roots that we must start; it is with Greek etymology, for "along with German, the Greek language is (in regard to its possibilities for thought) at once the most powerful and the most spiritual of all languages."

If we reach deeply enough into the origins of crucial Greek terms we may gain some sense of what grammar and perception were when "being" was still immediate to man, and we shall certainly gain some understanding of how it was that this immediacy came to be dissipated. The Greeks called "being" *ousia* or, more fully, *parousia*. Our dictionaries translate this word as "substance." Wrongly, says Heidegger. The veritable translation would be a set or cluster of significations comprising "homestead, at-homeness, a standing in and by itself, a self-enclosedness, an integral presentness or thereness." German *Anwesen* corresponds accurately to the range and force of meaning. *Parousia* tells us that "something is present to us. It stands firmly by itself and thus manifests and declares itself. It is. For the Greeks, 'being' basically meant this standing presence." Post-Socratic Greek thought, whether in Platonic idealism or Aristotelian substantiality, never returned to this pure and primal "ground of being," to this illumination of and through the presentness of the existing. But it is to just this ground that we must strive to come home ("homecoming" is, as we shall see, both the process and the goal of authentic being).

And if we embark seriously on the journey, a second linguistic marker of almost incalculable significance emerges (for Heidegger, the *figura etymologica*, the excavation of meaning from verbal roots and the history of words, is in the fullest sense an "emergence," a stepping into the light). We have seen that *ousia* signifies stable, enduring being. Being in its dynamic aspects is *physis* (the radical of our "physics"). Neither, says Heidegger, can be replaced by the term "existence." The latter is, when properly understood, the very opposite to "being." Ex-istence derives from a Greek source which means "to stand outside of," "to be in a posture external to" being. For the Greeks, so long as they were still in the light of *Dasein*, of immediate presentness, "existence" signified "nonbeing." "The thoughtless habit of using the words 'existence' and 'exist' as designations for being is one more indication of our estrangement both from being and from a radical, forceful, and definite exegesis of being." In many respects, *Sein und Zeit* is an attempt to separate the authenticity of "being" from the factitiousness of "existence." It is this same disjunction, urges Heidegger, which underlies the great distance between a true ontology (his own) and Sartre's existentialism.

But although this initial etymological foray has brought to light vital clues, it also confronts us with confusion. Between the dynamic abstraction of the infinitive "to be" and the apparently static verbal substantive "being" (*sein* and *das Sein*), contamination is unavoidable. Moreover, as we consider the verb, we notice at once that "I am" differs from "it is." In the immense majority of verbs, infinitive and present indicative are the same: "to say" and "I say," "to run" and "I run," "to love" and "I love."

But now we are up against a constellation which comprises "be," "am," "is," and "was." Why this plurality in what must surely be the most important, the most fundamental of all conjugations? We must dig deeper.

Again the probe is etymological. What are the linguistic roots of *sein*? Heidegger identifies three different stems. The first two are Indo-European. They turn up in the Greek and Latin words for "being." The oldest is *es*, Sanskrit *asus*, which Heidegger translates as *das Leben, das Lebende, das Eigenständige*, "life itself" ("the integral," "the autonomous"). To this "life-stem" belong Greek *esti*, Latin *est*, and German *ist*. So, of course, does English *is*. The second Indo-European radical is *bhu* or *bheu*. From it comes Greek *phuō*, "to emerge, to come to stand autonomously," as well as *physis* and *phyein* meaning, respectively, "nature" and "to grow." Heidegger conjectures that the *phy-* root also relates to the *pha-*, as in the Greek word *phainesthai*. The latter can be glossed as signifying "that which stands forth by entering into the light," "that which declares itself as a phenomenon." We shall see how important this conjecture is for Heidegger's view of science and technology, how vital it is to his attempts to provide phenomenology with a true ontological base. It is, in any event, from *phyein* that derive the Latin perfect *fui*, the English *be*, and German *bin* and *bist*. The third stem shows itself only when we inflect the German verb *sein*. Sanskrit *vasami* generates German *wesen*, an immensely polysemic word that Heidegger takes to mean "to dwell," "to sojourn," "to belong to and in." Hence *gewesen* ("to have been"), *war* ("was"), and what will become, especially for the later Heidegger, the key term *wesen* ("that which is in its active being," "that whose being is a manifest in-dwelling"). "From the three stems, we derive the three initial, concrete meanings: to live, to emerge, to linger or endure." (The archaic "perdure" might come closer to Heidegger's definition.)

But the upshot of our etymological and grammatical investigation is paradoxical. The infinitive and indicative status of the word "being" have been diluted. The word is now little more than a name for something indispensable yet almost entirely indeterminate. Etymology shows that three very different radicals are at work in *sein*. None of these three has come down to us with its numinous energy intact. What we have before us is a nebulous compromise. "Mixture and effacement go hand in hand." Are we back at our seemingly hollow or paralyzing starting point?

Not really. Heidegger now turns from semantic niceties to the rough-and-ready sovereignty of common experience. It may well be that the term "being" has become vacant or impenetrable. But things *are;* essents confront us on every hand. We discriminate between their being this way or that. We make immediate judgment as to whether something is or is not (this capacity to refer naturally and constantly to "nonbeing" will prove crucial). Asked to conceptualize for ourselves and for others, asked to define "tree," we could not and would not dream of doing so by merely enumerating and detailing an endless sequence of particular trees. In fact, we could not even identify any particular tree as belonging to the genus "tree" unless the notion of essence and its necessary implication of actual being were available to us. "Unless we are guided by a developed knowledge of treeness, which is manifestly determined from out of itself and its essential foundation, we can look at thousands and thousands of trees in vain—we shall not see the tree for the trees." Thus, although the word "being" is indefinite in meaning (or has become so), we grasp it with immediate definiteness. It is a certainty for us. And Heidegger notes polemically that it is in just so fundamental a case that formal and customary logic are an irrelevant construct.

A second challenge or dialectical consequence follows. It may be that we cannot provide for the term "being" an adequate syntactic analysis or paraphrase (an unambiguous, exhaustive definition). But being lives essentially in and through language. If we had no comprehension of being, if the word were "only a word"—as Heidegger's critics may argue—there could be no meaningful propositions whatever, no grammar, no predications. We would remain speechless. But "to be a man is to speak." Man says yes and no only because in his profound essence he is a speaker, *the* speaker. That is his distinction and at the same time his burden. It distinguishes him from stones, plants, animals, but also from the gods. Even if we had a thousand eyes and a thousand ears, a thousand hands and many other senses and organs, if our essence did not include the power of language, all essents would be closed to us, the essent that we ourselves are no less than the essent that we are not. For Heidegger, to be is "to speak being" or, more often, to question it. And it is precisely from the realization that "being" has at one and the same time an indefinite meaning and an overwhelmingly present one that our inquiry into "the thing itself" (Heidegger's idiom here is very nearly Kantian) must be conducted.

In *An Introduction to Metaphysics*, this inquiry, with its simultaneous assumption of opaqueness and self-evidence, concentrates on diverse usages of "is." Heidegger has no difficulty in showing that in such everyday locutions as "God is," "the book is mine," "the dog is in the garden," each "is" is meant differently. The attribution of being will always arise out of a definite situation,

purpose, mood (*Stimmung*), and "thereness" (*Dasein*).
In every "is," being discloses itself in a diversity of singular or combined ways. But in the grammar of essence,
with its triple roots and areas of overlap, "is" does occupy
a privileged rank. It is not in respect of "I am" that we
most readily and most assuredly seize on the nature of
being (here Heidegger differs fundamentally from the
"egoism" of Descartes and the subject-object fusion of
Kant and Fichte). Nor is it in respect of "you are" (as
certain modern schools of dialectical phenomenology
would have it). The grammatical category that dominates
our apprehension of being is the third-person singular or
the present indicative—"is." It is through "is" that we
conceptualize for ourselves the infinitive "to be." In German the collocation is immediate: *das Sein ist sein*. It is
this grammatical hierarchy, this articulate though usu-
ally unconscious third-person-singular ontology, which
has governed Western historical and philosophical consciousness and Western being since antiquity.

Heidegger goes on to analyze what he takes to be the
relation of "is" to a number of decisive "surrounding"
concepts. These are "becoming," "appearance," "thinking," and the notion of obligation in "ought." This analysis is conducted via seminal passages in Parmenides,
Pindar's Ninth Olympian Ode, fragments of Heraclitus,
and the celebrated first chorus from Sophocles' *Antigone*
(332–75). These readings are intended to demonstrate
how the Greek experience of being, in its pre-Socratic
phase and in its great moments of "thinking poetry" (*des
dichtenden Denkens*), must remain the touchstone and
starting point for that question of being which will determine the worth and, quite literally, the survival of
modern man. Heidegger's return to origins, whether in the
etymology of a word or in the stream of thought, is not,
as we have already seen, an arbitrary or pedantic archa-

ism (though there are elements of both in his work). It is, at its best, the expression of a deeply meditated conviction that in human thought, as in all important phenomena, "the beginning is the strangest and mightiest."

Each of the examined texts, moreover, confirms the indissoluble links between being and speech. "Simultaneously with man's departure into being, he finds himself in the word, in language." Invoking Heraclitus, Heidegger will give to *logos* and to *legein* a very particular sense: that of "collecting," "ordered gathering," and a "laying side by side." (But the Johannine formula, "In the beginning was the Word," is obviously present in his whole paradigm of being and saying.) Thus the notorious enigma of the origins of human speech is grounded in the phenomenon and temporality of man's entrance into being. In a turn of phrase strikingly reminiscent of Vico, the pioneer of modern historicism, Heidegger writes: "Language is the primordial poetry in which a people speaks being. Conversely, the great poetry by which a people enters into history initiates the molding of its language. The Greeks created and experienced this poetry through Homer. Language was made manifest to their being-there [*Da-sein*] as departure into being, as a configuration disclosing the essent."

A scrutiny of the Greek language in its early, pristine stages, a scrutiny which begins with etymology but strives to become a full "re-experiencing" of the life within and around words, will help us to locate, to "undergo" *ousia*— that decisive term for being with which our questioning began. Already, we have achieved a number of insights. The permanence of being stands in opposition to the flux of becoming. That which is actually seen to be stands opposed to the changing appearance of the seeming. It is thought, not the eye, that distinguishes between permanence and motion, between essence and appearance.

Therefore, there is a sense in which thought, *dianoia,* and thought alone, actualizes both being and what is opposed to being: "Thought is the sustaining and determining ground of being" (a proposition we might find in Fichte). But "ground" entails a downward movement (Heidegger, in fact, uses a simple diagram). As soon as being realizes itself as an "idea," as soon as essence is "idealized," the arrow points upward. It points, inevitably, to "ought," to the category of the exemplary, the prototypical, the teleological and obligatory. In the realm of "ideas," essents are endowed with a purpose, a forward-directed rationality, a "should." This conjunction of futurity and obligation is the core of Platonic and Kantian idealism.

Thus we find ourselves saddled with a fourfold distinction as between "being," "becoming," "thought," and the "higher" sphere of "idea" and "ought." This foursome has permeated Western philosophy (metaphysics) and history. But if one is to ask the "beingquestion" radically, says Heidegger, one must thoroughly rethink these categories, recognizing both their power and error. One must compel them back to their forgotten source. If we do so, we shall see that this fourfold theme does indeed "dominate and bewitch the essent, its disclosure and configuration." *But it does not define it.* The sense of being that has governed philosophy and ordinary language since Plato "does not suffice to name everything that 'is.'" Neither idealism, even in its rigorous phenomenological guise, nor scientific positivism comes anywhere near to a convincing grasp of "isness." *Sein und Zeit* shows us that such grasp depends on understanding the difference between "Being" and "beings," between "Being" and "essents." But such understanding cannot spring from thought alone. Or, more precisely, in the Heideggerian sense, "to think Being" one must "live it." The cardinal concepts are not "Being and Thought," as they are in Plato, Descartes, and

authentic questioning is a correspondence, an *Entsprechen*. It accords with, it is a responsion to the essence of that *after* which it inquires (*dem Wesen dessen nach dem gefragt wird*). In this phrasing, "after," *nach*, carries undeniable overtones of attendance upon, circumspect effacement before. Heidegger's questioner is the very contrary of a Baconian inquisitor.

The talk of *Wissenschaft und Besinnung* ("Science/ Knowledge and Reflection"), which Heidegger gave in August 1953, further elaborates this methodological and moral interaction of question and answer. A seminal distinction is made between what is merely *fraglich*, "questionable," and what is *fragwürdig*, "worthy of being questioned." The "questionable" (English reproduces the pejorative inflection) pertains to the ontologically secondary, to the contingent, to the pragmatic or even trivial spheres of positive investigation. In this sphere, which we might compare with Mr. Gradgrind's world of "facts," there are terminal answers, decidabilities of a kind that leave the question "settled" and, therefore, inert. There is really not very much to be gained from asking yet again what is the mileage to the moon or which is the formula for making hydrochloric acid. We *know* the answers, and the finality of this knowledge has, according to Heidegger, demonstrated the in-essentiality or, at the last, smallness of the original question. That which is "worthy of questioning," on the other hand, is literally inexhaustible. There are no terminal answers, no last and formal decidabilities to the question of the meaning of human existence or of a Mozart sonata or of the conflict between individual conscience and social constraint. The *Fragwürdige* dignifies the question and the questioner by making of the process of interrogation and response an ever-renewed dialogue and counterpoint. But if there can be no end to genuine questioning, the process is, nonetheless, not aimless. "The wandering," says Heidegger, "the peregrination toward that which is worthy of being questioned, is not adventure but homecoming." Man, in his dignity, comes home to the unanswerable. And that, of course, which is most *fragwürdig* is "Being."

But can we get no closer to this absolutely determining, all-pervading word? Is Heidegger's existential ontology expressive only in terms of elusive circularity?

Heidegger wrote his *Letter on "Humanism"* in 1945–46. He was under obvious political and personal pressures. He was at pains to dissociate his own teachings from what he regarded as a Sartrean perversion. This may be the reason why the *Letter* comes nearer than any other Heideggerian text, except for the last four retrospective colloquia, to spelling out the meaning, to delimiting the field of proper reference, of "Being" and "being":

> *Doch das Sein—was ist das Sein? Es ist Es selbst. Dies zu erfahren und zu sagen, muss das künftige Denken lernen. Das "Sein"—das ist nicht Gott und nicht ein Weltgrund. Das Sein ist weiter denn alles Seiende und ist gleichwohl dem Menschen näher als jedes Seiende, sei dies ein Fels, ein Tier, ein Kunstwerk, eine Maschine, sei es ein Engel oder Gott. Das Sein ist das Nächste. Doch die Nähe bleibt dem Menschen am weitestem.* [But Being—what is Being? It is itself. Future thinking, thought that is to come, must learn to experience this and to say it. Being—is not God and not a foundation for or final abyss of the world. Being is at once further from man than all beings, and nearer than all essents, be they a rock, an animal, a work of art, a machine, be they an angel or God. Being is the nearest to man. But this nearness remains furthest from him.]

Here we find ourselves, as it were, at the still center of Martin Heidegger's entire work and thought. "Being *is*." It is the quiddity, the essence, the "isness" in every particular essent and in every statement of existence, i.e., in every act of speech. "Being is"; *il y a l'Etre*. Heidegger cites both, and both are correct. But neither English nor French can fully equate the German formulation: *es gibt Sein* or *es gibt das Sein*. Literally and, so far as English goes, unacceptably, German says: "it gives Being." For Heidegger, this "it" that "gives" is Being itself, and the fusion of "Being" with "giving" or "being given" is immensely important. (Anglo-American slang can almost get it right: "What *gives* with you?" signifies "How are things with you?") Here also, it is language itself which speaks, and it is we who must, by scrupulous attendance (by "going after" it), learn what it has to tell us. What *it* is saying—not, primarily, what we are saying or offering in reply.

If this formulation of *Sein* appears to be inadequate, vacuous, mystical—in *Zur Seinsfrage* Heidegger fully acknowledges that the Western, metaphysically and positivistically schooled intellect will derive this impression from it—this may well be because our speaking is not yet a "saying." Its relations to being are still those of forgetting and of aggressive determinism. It is *das künftige Denken,* the "thought that is still to come" which will be able to experience and to say being, which will see in apparent tautology the organon of truth. The "definition" of "Being" put forward in the *Letter on "Humanism"* is no more than a "marker" on the forest way (*Wegmarken am Holzweg*).

But is this good enough? Should a marker, however tentative, in a forest, however obscure, not point to something beyond itself, to something of which external verification is conceivable? In other words: Has Heidegger actually told us anything about "Being" and "being"; has he communicated to us any content or method of understanding susceptible of either support or refutation? Or are his "predefinitions," his latent metaphors, his models of inward-circling query and response rigorously "insignificant" and, at bottom, of a kind with the mantras of the mystic and the self-hypnotized? We saw at the outset that numerous philosophers, beginning with Carnap and the logical positivists, would say just this. Heidegger is a mouther of emptiness, particularly at this central point in his ontology or purported dialectic of being. This is not, I repeat, a finding that can be peremptorily dismissed or reduced to mere professional myopia. It is a critique and counterstatement which should be kept steadily in view, however problematic it makes the obvious dimension, the intense presence of Heidegger's example and writings in current reference and sensibility. It *may* be that Heidegger's "saying of being," however fervently invoked by disciples and sympathizers, signifies nothing or does not translate out of its own autistic rapture. (This would still leave open the cardinal issue as to whether Heidegger's questions are or are not worth asking, whether they are or are not the most important questions posed to man.)

There is a second way of looking at the case. It can and has been argued that the Heideggerian doctrine of essence and existence is—despite its explicit profession and contrary purpose—no more than a variation on the dominant motifs and vocabulary of Western metaphysics. Far from accomplishing a radical break with the past, an overthrow of all precedent epistemology, Heidegger on *Sein* and *das Seiende* would be a restatement of axioms and discriminations pervasive in Western thought from Plato to Kant and Husserl. Thus the distinction between existential particulars and that which is the essence of their and of all existence would be a reformulation of the central Platonic distinction between the phenomenal and the ideal, between the visible realm of contingent singularity and the invisible but "real" world of Ideas.

Heidegger's stress on being as an activity, as a noun "in" or "through" the infinitive of the verb, *das Wesen welches west* (an essence in process), would closely approximate the Aristotelian notion of *energeia* and the Aristotelian doctrine of a shaping force whose teleological drive animates all specific essents. It is these Aristotelian representations which generate the world-picture and logic of medieval scholasticism in which the young Heidegger had been steeped. Consequently, his "being" (*das Seiende*) would correspond to the *ens per accidente*, the contingent state of things, whereas "Being" (*das Sein* or *das Sein des Seienden*) could be equated with the scholastic and Thomistic *ens tamquam verum*, "that which really is." Descartes's *cogito* and Fichte's *Ich* would anticipate that irreducible "being-in-the-world" which Heidegger posits as the source and locus of human experience. Kant's dissociation between that which is accessible to analytic perception and the *Ding an sich*, "the thing in itself," would be the obvious model for Heidegger's dualism. Hegel's *Geist*, or "Spirit," would prefigure Heideggerian "Being," as would Nietzsche's hypostatization of Will. And in Edmund Husserl's phenomenological reductionism, in his insistence on the intentional structure of all thought and perceiving (to think is to think of something), one would find the core of Heidegger's facticity, of the great evocation in *Sein and Zeit* of all "that lies to hand."

Seen in this light, Heidegger's repeated critique of each of these philosophers and of the systematic unfolding of Western thought as it is set out in their teachings is at best tactical and, at worst, self-deceiving; the distinction between "Being" and "being" or "beings" is, in fact, yet one more phrasing of that binary edifice of understanding and of the correlative attempt to proceed from the apparent to the real, from the mobile to the unmoving, from the sensory to the purely intelligible, which have been the lofty routine of all Western metaphysics and theories of cognition after Socrates.

We shall see how strenuously Heidegger rejects this accommodation, how sharply he underlines what he takes to be the rupture between his own ontology and that of all post-Socratic philosophic discourse. Nevertheless he is sensible to the charge that he has done no more than wrap old suppositions in novel jargon. If *Sein und Zeit* remains incomplete (the late lecture on *"Zeit und Sein"* being no more than a fragment of an intended whole), it is, says Heidegger, because his idiom, however dark and idiosyncratic, remains charged with the presumptions and tonalities of traditional metaphysics. It is because he was unable to find the language needed to overcome the vocabulary, the grammar, the semantic implications and constraining conventions of Western metaphysical argument. The search for a new poetics of statement in Heidegger's writings during and after World War II is the immediate result of this realization of defeat. Even the primordial terms *Sein* and *das Seiende* had remained inwoven in that Platonic idealism or scholastic categorization or Cartesian subjectivity or Nietzschean voluntarism in which Heidegger saw the false, though unavoidable, turn of Western philosophy away from the authentic, numinous fonts of being. Heidegger tells us that he is saying something profoundly new and different (though what he is saying is, at an even deeper level, a re-cognition, a homecoming); but he is the first to suggest that the language available to him is inadequate to his demands.

There is a third attack possible. There may well be a Heideggerian doctrine or picture of being. But it is not philosophy at all. Heidegger was schooled as a theologian and remained one. His teaching constitutes a sort of metatheology whose language is immersed, inescapably, in that of Pietism, scholasticism, and Lutheran doxology. Consider the all-governing tautology: *Was ist das Sein? Es ist es selbst.* What we have here is quite patently an imitation of the equivalence fundamental to the Judeo-Christian definition of God: "I am that which I am." The Heideggerian postulate of a language speaking "in and through" man is an immediate borrowing from the Johannine doctrine of the *Lógos* and its long legacy in Western mystical-Pietist expression. When Heidegger qualifies man as the "shepherd of being," when he sees truth as an illumination, an epiphany and self-disclosure in the "clearing" of existence, he is varying on long-established theological and gnostic themes. His repeated conviction that the enterprise of philosophy is that of a pilgrimage *toward,* that the journey already enfolds within itself what we can grasp of its fulfillment, represents a precise simile to the religious figure of man's journey and to the religious-meditational striving after transcendence.

What we really find in Heidegger's work, therefore, is one of a number of postdoctrinal, postsystematic theologies. The just grounds for comparison would be neither with the Aristotelian categories of the existential nor with Husserl's search for scientific certitude, but with Kierkegaard's ironic eschatology or the new gospel of *Thus Spake Zarathustra.* Whence the fact that it was the theologians who were the first to take up *Sein und Zeit,* and that it is on theologians and those who metaphorize theologically (like certain psychiatrists and poets) that Heidegger's impact has, until now, been most incisive.

Heidegger protests vehemently against this allocation. He declares tirelessly that his propositions on "Being" entail absolutely nothing as to the existence or nonexistence of God. He urges that the epistemology and theory of being set forth in *Sein und Zeit* and the *Letter on "Human-*

ism" are an explicit rejoinder to what he calls the "onto-theological" bias in Western thinking. Whereas the latter arrives, inherently, at the inference of the transcendent, at the attempt to locate truth and ethical values in some abstract "beyond," Heidegger's ontology is densely immanent. Being is being-in-the-world. There "is" nowhere else. Being and authenticity can only be realized within immanent existence and time. For Heidegger, there is no divine sphere of immaculate ideation, no unmoved mover.

All this is certainly true of *Sein und Zeit,* and of Heidegger's critique of an infinite regress toward transcendence in the theories of reality and understanding in Aristotle, in Kant, in the Hegelian dialectic. Nonetheless, the substitution of "the One," of "the First Principle," of "the Absolute" or, simply, of "God" for *Sein* and the *Sein des Seienden* in many key passages in Heidegger's texts is undeniably plausible. Time and again the whole tenor of argument, the resort to an undefinable immediacy of cognition, the close analogy to scriptural and notably Pauline turns of homily and rhetoric carry a theological charge. So, as we shall see, does Heidegger's entire hermeneutic, or technique of textual exegesis and metaphrase. Here, as well, the strangeness of Heidegger's later style and the striking recourse to the antique gods may represent an attempt to escape from a theological precedent, from an informing origin in theological speech and feeling, even more powerful than was that of metaphysics. Heidegger affirms that " 'Being' is not God." Unmistakably, however, its sufficiency unto itself, its ubiquity "nearest to" and "furthest from" man, have a marked theological edge.

One's judgment as to whether Heidegger's "thinking of being" is mesmeric bluff, an esoteric variant on long-established metaphysical and epistemological motifs, a concealed theology, or a composite of all three, does have real intellectual and political consequences. This is the fascination of the case. But such a judgment can be arrived at only by the individual reader, immersing himself in the pertinent texts on a scale far beyond that of this short introduction. The best to be done here is to see how Heidegger's own followers and interpreters summarize and apply the main postulates and corollaries of the *Seinsfrage*. Among the most qualified and sympathetic of Heidegger's readers are the French philosopher Emmanuel Lévinas, in *En Découvrant l'existence avec Husserl et Heidegger*, and, as I already mentioned, Fr. William J. Richardson, S.J., whose *Heidegger: Through Phenomenology to Thought* remains pre-eminent in the field. It cannot be an accident that both proceed from a theological background. Accepting their lead, we get something like the following précis.

From 1907 on, when he had read Brentano on Aristotle, Heidegger had posed the question: "What is the 'Being' which renders possible all existence, which is the *is* in every essent?" Almost at once, he took the next step. If it is "Being" (*Sein*) that makes present, that makes extant all particular beings, is it not the fundamental and compelling task of philosophy, of serious thought insofar as it characterizes man's humanity, to inquire into "Being" itself, to ask what *it is*? Heidegger soon observed that there is indeed a sense in which all Western metaphysics has asked this very same question. It is inherent in the word metaphysics, which signifies a "going beyond nature," an attempt to transcend discrete phenomenal units in order to arrive at the universal principles of reality and existence that lie "inside" or "beyond" them. This attempt is crucial to Plato's distinction, in the celebrated parable of the Cave, between the shadow-beings of sensory experience and the essential, unaltering realm of Ideas. We have noted how this distinction, variously phrased, runs through the entirety of Western thought. But here comes Heidegger's revolutionary dissent and innovation. Very early on, in his study of Platonic and Kantian idealism, of Aristotelian and scholastic doctrines of substance, of Leibnizian determinism and Hegelian dialectic, Heidegger became convinced that the whole motion of metaphysics toward transcendence was circular and self-deceiving. By calling the presence of "Being" in "beings" "Ideas" or "energy" or "Spirit" or "*élan vital*" (Bergson's term), metaphysicians had merely substituted one occult essent or existential causation for another. What have we gained by positing an inaccessible domain of pure forms above and beyond the tangible world, or by ascribing to all sensible phenomena a hidden teleological agency (the respective Platonic and Aristotelian paradigms)? Heidegger's proceeding will be entirely different.

Instead of making of singular, phenomenal, objective beings—the things and presences that furnish our world —the degenerate fragments of a Platonic ideal sphere or the fluctuating matrix for intangible Aristotelian energies, Heidegger concentrates on the total *thereness* of these particular existentials. They fill him with wonder. He stands soul- and spirit-deep in immanence, in that which is, and in the utter strangeness and wonder of his own "isness" within it. But what, then, is it which enables beings, with all their dense and silent quiddity—the rock, the tree, the animal looking at us—to offer themselves to that act of fundamental astonishment which is the necessary source of philosophic questioning? Heidegger answers: the presence of all that is present (present *to us*) is made possible by virtue of an illumination, a "being lit" (does this shorthand derive from Fichte's use of "light"?) that renders every inorganic and organic thing "unconcealed." The word is *unverborgen*, another key term. But this light itself does remain concealed. *It is not itself a being*—or "Idea" or "energy" or "*Ding an sich*" or "Spirit." It is that by which all beings shine forth—and it is precisely in the word *phenomenon* that Heidegger finds a Greek root meaning "radiance," "self-disclosure." He could also have cited the Cabala, which conceives of the Deity as self-concealed *in* all things, yet as revealed, as made radiant *by* them.

But what is this "light," this hidden source of un-hiddenness? Since Plato, says Heidegger, Western metaphysics has not asked this question, or where it has intimated it, as in Kant, it has failed to press it home. Heidegger will ask nothing else. We saw his tautological reply in the *Letter on "Humanism."* Here is Richardson's gloss:

> Being is not a being, because it is that which enables beings to be present to man and men to each other. It is nearest to man, because it makes him to be what he is and enables him to enter into comportment with other beings. Yet it is farthest removed from him because it is not a being with which he, structured as he is to deal directly with only beings, can comport himself.

Lévinas's summary proceeds from a less anthropomorphic starting point. Heidegger differentiates between whatever is (*das Seiende, l'étant*) and *das Sein des Seienden* or *l'être de l'étant*.

> Whatever is, *l'étant*, comprises the sum-total of all things, of all persons, in a certain sense it comprises God Himself. The Being of beings, *l'être de l'étant*, is the fact that all these objects and persons *are*. Being does not identify itself with any of these beings, not even with the concept of being in general. In a certain sense, Being is not (*il n'est pas*). For if Being were, it would in its turn be a being: *il serait étant à son tour*,

whereas Being is, in some way, the very occurrence of existence in and of all beings, *l'événement même d'être de tous les étants.*

The Being of being(s) is the only proper object of ontological thought. The world of beings is investigated by what Heidegger calls the *ontic* sciences. Geology studies the attributes, material composition, and history of rocks. Ontology tries to "think the being of the rock," tries to experience that which gives it existence or, more precisely, how it is that existence manifests itself in the rock. But this is not to devalue the substantive world, as does Platonic idealism, Cartesian subjectivity, Kantian transcendence, or Nietzschean voluntarism. On the contrary, it is to immerse oneself in the full "thereness" of things; for it is only in their unconcealment that Being, though itself hidden, is revealed. Every inanimate and animate presence, ontologically wondered at and thought "through"—"through" assuming a palpable force of penetration—becomes a "clearing," a *Lichtung* in which Being declares itself—like the light that plays around objects in the dark of the wood even though we cannot place its source. The light itself is neither subject nor object: it is a process, a *Wesen* or, as Richardson puts it, "a to-be." And as we struggle with such a notion or such an incipient metaphor, Heidegger reminds us of the fact that our normal habits of speech, of definitional logic, of causal relation and verifiability are grounded in just those metaphysical presuppositions and determinants which he is attempting to overthrow. No wonder we do not "understand" fully; if we did, we would already have come home to Being.

Being does not—it cannot, we are told—reveal itself outside the being in which it lodges and which it illumines. "Being," says Richardson, "contracts into the beings it makes manifest and hides by the very fact that it reveals." This Being itself *is not,* not in or of itself. This is Heidegger's central paradox and source of meditation. From 1929 onward, he emphasized more and more that this hiddenness of Being must entail the reality of non-Being, that Being is, in the final analysis, an emergence, an epiphany out of Nothingness (*Nichts*). The latter is, therefore, no vacant abstraction. The point is vital and obscure. Let us follow closely.

There could be no experience of Being, such as we manifestly have, unless Being were hidden in beings, in the essents which comprise man and the world. It is precisely this negative character of Being, the fact that Being is not an entity in itself (the Kantian *Ding an sich*), which generates the powers of manifestation in beings. It is hidden Being that gives the rock its dense "thereness," that makes the heart pause when a kingfisher alights, that makes our own existence inseparable from that of others. In each case, wonder and reflection tell us of an intensity of presentness, an integral unfolding or self-statement, *clearly in excess of sensory data and neutral registration.* The sum *is* so obviously greater, "more there" than the parts. There *is* so much more in front of us than meets the eye or hand or analytic brain. To grasp it we must think dialectically, we must understand how the negative, the hidden, the "not-there" can engender the manifest and positive. "Being as the process of non-concealments," explains Richardson, "is that which permits beings to become non-concealed (positivity), although the process is so permeated by 'not' that Being itself remains concealed (negativity)." To this process of concealment which brings forth openness, as the chemical medium, invisible in the darkroom, brings forth the picture, Heidegger gives the Greek name for truth, *aletheia* ("the un-concealed").

Why, then, is it that Western metaphysics has forgotten Being, why has it labored to efface or sublimate the absolutely fundamental difference between Being and beings, between *Sein* and *Seienden*? The trap, says Heidegger, was there from the first. The Greek word for "being," *on* (archaic *eon* in the *Iliad*, I, 70), was ambiguous. It could signify either "being" in the infinitive sense of "to be," or "being" in the nominal sense of "a being," most notably "a supreme being." Inevitably, this ambiguity led away from an authentic "thinking of and on Being" to Heidegger's "onto-theology," an attempt to found the meaning and reality of existence in some ultimate principle or divine agent. The Socratic-Platonic distinction between sensible and suprasensible, the Aristotelian chain of being which leads from brute matter to an unmoving mover and First Cause, the explicit theology of the Thomists, the god of Descartes who is guarantor of rationality, are direct consequences of the original muddle.

When Leibniz asked, "Why is there being at all and not much rather non-being?" he was posing the authentic question as it had first been voiced by Parmenides and by Heraclitus. But by the mid-seventeenth century it was too late. In Plato the Ideas are both the source of light and the only true thing-to-be-seen. This truth comes to mean accurate perception, and Being is thereby reduced to beings. Rationality, in both Plato and Aristotle, is the conformity between cognizance and object. The Scholastics, thoroughly Aristotelian in this regard, will simply add that this conformity is underwritten by God. The next step is Descartes's, who strives to make the conformity between *ratio* and object a verifiable, scientific certitude underwritten by God, ultimately, but guaranteed more immediately by the structure of mathematics. Beings are only true insofar as they enter into the polarized bond of rational subject and verifiable object. In Descartes, says Heidegger pointedly, transcendence becomes "rescendence." Everything is referred back to the human viewer. The *cogito* comes before the *sum;* thought precedes being; and truth is a function of the certitude of the human subject.

Leibniz's monads, each endowed with perception and appetite, are an ingenious extension of the Cartesian *ego.* What Kant does in his critiques is to analyze and elucidate the conditions needed if the subject is to have a proper perception of the object. In Hegel, subjectivity and subjective idealism culminate in a kind of absolute certainty which, says Heidegger, is no more than a dynamic solipsism. The nihilism of Nietzsche was the inevitable closing chapter in the history of metaphysics. The old Platonic and theological values are dead, as is the absolute in Kantian ethics and the autistic confidence in Hegelian historicism. But for all its lyric magnetism, the Nietzschean Will-to-Power is itself only a wildly exalted subjectivity. And from it flows that impulse, which defines the modern situation, to dominate the earth through scientific classification and technological use. If man does not learn to overcome this imperialist subjectivity, he is doomed. But such learning means that he must return to the sources of his humanity, that he must begin to rethink "the sense of Being" (*den Sinn des Seins zu denen*).

To rethink in this way, a man must repudiate not only his metaphysical inheritance and the seductions of "technicity," but also the egocentric humanism of liberal enlightenment and, finally, logic itself. For logic also is caught in, is the custodian of, the old metaphysical trap that sees truth as conformity with subjective, rational cognizance. True ontological thought, as Heidegger conceives it, is presubjective, prelogical and, above all, open to Being. It *lets Being be* (the operative German term is *Sein-lassen*). In this "letting-be" man does play a very important part, but it is only a part.

Man alone "ex-ists" in the very concrete sense that he alone can "think Being." The tree, the rock, God *is*, says Heidegger, but does not exist if we understand by existence the capacity of man to stand outside himself (whence the hyphen in "ex-ist"), to make himself ecstatically open to the radiance of Being, a stance to which the etymological links between "ex-istence" and "ecstasy" are a clue. "The understanding of Being," writes Lévinas, "is the determining attribute and fundamental fact of human existence." Man, he goes on, is "a being who understands Being" (*un étant qui comprend l'être*). But this understanding is not an ancillary or contingent enterprise. It is that which gives to man's being its whole meaning and humanity: "*Cette compréhension de l'être est elle-même l'être; elle n'est pas un attribut, mais le mode d'existence de l'homme.*" Thus, as we shall see when we come to Heidegger's views on language, poetry, and art, there is a pivotal sense in which Being does require man, for it is in him that it finds its privileged "clearing." Hence also the conclusion that to "think on and of Being," to practice philosophy in the manner which Heidegger will derive from the pre-Socratics, from Meister Eckhardt, from Hölderlin's odes, from van Gogh's painting of a pair of peasant shoes, is not a professional, specialized, occasional pursuit. It is the condition of any authentic personal life and its most intimate event. ("*La philosophie,*" summarizes Lévinas, "*est la condition de la vie, elle en est l'événement le plus intime.*")

This, in rough outline, is Martin Heidegger's ontology

and "counter-metaphysic." How does it apply to problems of daily existence, of moral choice, of personal and collective psychology? To answer, we must look to *Sein und Zeit,* and later to the politics that came six years after its publication.

Being and Time

11

The period 1916–27 constitutes the spell of creative silence in Heidegger's development. Many
aspects of this period remain unclear, but the
main lines of personal experience and intellectual
contact can be traced. Heidegger works with Husserl, whom he will succeed at Freiburg in 1928,
and masters the mental discipline and vocabulary
of phenomenology, of the search for a firm basis
for perception and cognition in acts of pure consciousness. Karl Barth's commentary on *The
Epistle to the Romans* appears in 1918. It influences Heidegger's whole style of textual exposition, of word-by-word interpretation, and directs
his attention to the radical, psychologizing theology of Kierkegaard. This theological interest,
from 1923 on, brings Heidegger into close exchange with Bultmann, and forms the basis for
a persistent mutual awareness between Heideg-

gerian ontology and the modern "theology of crisis" and de-mythologization. It is during these years, moreover, that Heidegger studies and lectures on texts from Saint Augustine, the entire Pauline corpus, and Luther. Together with Pascal, whose portrait hangs on the wall of his study, these are the crucial sources for Heidegger's concepts of *Angst* ("anguish"), of conscience as reality-principle, and of the individuation of death.

At the same time, Heidegger is much influenced by Dilthey's theory of history and by Dilthey's attempt to define the true relations between human consciousness and historical fact. It is from Dilthey that Heidegger seems to derive his fundamental and surely evaluative distinction between the technical (ontic) truths of the exact and applied sciences, and the orders of authentic insight aimed at in the historical and "spiritual" sciences, the *Geisteswissenschaften*. The correspondence between Dilthey and the Graf von Yorck, with its debate on the nature of intuition and temporality, is published in 1923 and will figure importantly in *Sein und Zeit*. Dilthey and Yorck, together with the argument on the nature of historicity, are instrumental in Heidegger's insistence on the temporal determination and boundedness of human existence. The embedding of man's identity in history is, of course, a cardinal feature of Hegelian and revolutionary Marxism. To a degree which has become visible only recently (and to which I will return), Heidegger is, throughout the 1920s, fully cognizant of the philosophic-ideological debates being pursued in the German and Central European Marxist movements. In particular, he knows the early works of George Lukács. He shares with the Lukács of *Die Seele und die Formen* (1911) an interest in Kierkegaard and in the psychological and literary models of human consciousness initiated by Nietzsche's writing. He has in common with the Lukács of *History and Class Consciousness* (first published in Germany in 1923) a commitment to the concrete, historically existential quality of human acts of perception and intellection.

Even more telling, perhaps, though difficult to gauge so long as personal archives remain closed, is the impact on Heidegger of World War I and of the moral and economic debacle of Weimar Germany. Though he later evolved his own, very special reading of Western history as a *Seinsvergessenheit*, a "forgetting of Being" which deflects Western man from his authentic mission after Plato, there can be little doubt that Heidegger was influenced by the Spenglerian scenario of the fatal decline of the West (volume I of Spengler's treatise appeared in 1918). This crepuscular vision found violent echo and analogy in the art and poetry of expressionism. A characteristically entitled anthology of Expressionist verse, *Menschheitsdämmerung* (*Mankind's Twilight*), edited by Kurt Pintus, was published in 1921. We know that it marked Heidegger's whole view of poetry, and it may well have prepared his later uses of Rilke and Trakl. Like his Expressionist contemporaries, Heidegger saw in Dostoevski and van Gogh the ultimate masters of spiritual truth, of vision in and into depths. This assessment, in turn, accords with the crisis-theology he found in Pascal and in Kierkegaard. Though his personal role had not been an active one, the mere fact of an insanely destructive, internecine European war and of its revolutionary aftermath justified, if justification was needed, the notion of man and culture *in extremis*, of final inauthenticity, of a descent into nihilism. It bore out the impotence of Cartesian-Kantian rational confidence, and the apocalyptic obsessions to be found in the great solitary artists, theologians, thinkers of the nineteenth century. Thus there is a distinct sense in which *Sein und Zeit*, for all its erratic singularity, does belong to the same climate of catastrophe and the same quest for alternative vision as do T. S. Eliot's *The Waste Land* or Hermann Hesse's *Blick ins Chaos* with which it is so nearly contemporary.

But once we have sought to clarify the relevant philosophic, theological, social, literary, and personal circumstances in Heidegger's early development, and once we have marked substantial points of reference to Husserl, to Kierkegaard, to Dilthey, to the Hegelian-Marxists and to expressionism, we have still said very little about the actual shaping of *Sein und Zeit*. The shock felt, and borne witness to, by its first readers when it appeared almost casually in Husserl's phenomenological yearbook for 1927 is with us still. The psychologist and philosopher O. F. Bollnow speaks for many when he applies to *Sein und Zeit* Goethe's famous dictum after the battle of Valmy: "From today and from here on, a new epoch has begun in world history, and you can say that you were present at its beginning." Within half a year of publication, Heidegger's notoriety in philosophic and theological circles was assured. By 1930, the secondary literature was extensive. Heidegger's repeated statement that the manuscript had been more or less taken away from him (for motives of academic promotion) and that the work, as it stood, was a fragment, added to the general sense of strangeness and revelation. So, to be sure, did his refusal to elucidate or comment on its "meanings." But even apart from historical and personal circumstance, it can fairly be said that there is, in the history of Western thought, no other work like *Sein und Zeit*.

At one level, this is obviously true of any significant philosophic text: of Pascal's *Pensées*, of Hegel's *Phenomenology*, of Wittgenstein's *Tractatus*. Each is the generator of its own unique terms of reference. But with *Sein und Zeit* the deliberate singularity seems even more intense. It extends to every feature of style, argumentative construction, and stated intention. The meaning is totally in the manner, the manner is, in every technical and tonal aspect, integral to the meaning. An essentialist fusion of this order of inner necessity and formal uniqueness characterizes great poetry and art. It is extremely rare, indeed suspect, within the framework of discursive, outwardly "academic" philosophic prose. The achievement of this fusion, by stylistic means, does relate *Sein und Zeit* to the *Phenomenology* and to the *Tractatus*. It relates it also to Nietzsche's *Genealogy of Morals*. In order to construe its appropriate propositional idiom and inner architecture, each of these books had to break with the approved professional models of philosophic exposition, of logical proof, of critique. In each, consequently, there are psychological dramatizations and rhetorical motives which interest the student of language and of poetics as closely as they do the philosopher or logician. The presence of Hegel's *Phenomenology* and Nietzsche's critique of values in Heidegger's *Sein und Zeit* is organic. That of the *Tractatus* is uncertain, but a case has been made for it. Together, Heidegger's and Wittgenstein's treatises are postulates of rigorous inception; they are attempts to begin all over again. The question of how to read them, of what a genuine reading entails, not merely in terms of analytic grasp but—and this is what matters to both authors—in terms of a recomposition of the reader's values and conduct, remains as challenging as when the two texts first appeared (each in a fairly recondite journal).

The best I can hope to do is to try to set out a number of the main issues and formulations in the order in which they are advanced in *Sein und Zeit*, and with reference to the general sketch of Heidegger's vocabulary provided in chapter 1. Even so pedestrian a way should lead toward and evoke something of that *helle Nacht* (Hölderlin's phrase for a lit and lighting dark) which readers have experienced for over half a century.

The title is a manifesto. Traditionally, *Sein* is timeless. In metaphysics after Plato, the investigation of being, of the essence within or behind appearance, is precisely a quest for that which is constant, which stands eternal in the flux of time and change. Heidegger's title proclaims otherwise: *Sein und Zeit*. Being is itself temporal (*zeitlich*)—as it is with reference to the specificity in time of the Incarnation and of Christ's return in *Thessalonians*, I; as it is also in Book X of Saint Augustine's *Confessions* and in some of the Gnostics on whom Heidegger lectured in the summer term of 1921; as it is, again, in the emphasis of the young Luther on the immersion of the individual soul in the time-bound medium of factual-historical experience. We do not live "in time," as if the latter were some independent, abstract flow external to our being. We "live time"; the two terms are inseparable. *Sein und Zeit* sets out to demonstrate this stringent unity (as we have it, the book in fact does so only incompletely). But the conjunction in the title is all-important.

It has been the fatal error of approved metaphysical thinking to envisage *Sein* as some sort of eternal presentness or *Vorhandensein*, "out there." Already Augustine had warned against the obsessive *concupiscentia oculorum* of philosophers, their Platonic insistence on "seeing" the essence of things instead of experiencing it with total existential commitment and patience—which commitment entails a realization of the time-bound nature of being. Hegel's dialectic and Nietzsche's voluntarism compound this error. Inevitably, *Sein* has been "seen," that is to say imagined, abstracted, metaphorized, all of which visual appropriation are equally spurious. They make of being a mere *Gegenwart*, a kind of objective entity "out

there." Such "objective viewing" uproots man. It con-
signs him to curiosity (*Neugier*, literally "lust for novelty") and self-scattering. "Reification," "alienation," "one-
dimensionality" are now the fashionable tags for this
unhoused and kaleidoscopic condition.

It is, on the contrary, the Augustinian-Kierkegaardian
stress (itself ultimately Pauline) on man's rootedness in
the concrete, temporal world, and the Pascalian-Lutheran
stress on *Angst*, with its affirmation of the nearness and
time-governing presentness of death, that fuse *Sein und
Zeit* into necessary oneness. Instead of the Platonic "illumination from outside," with its archetypal figure of
the eye reaching out to an object along an exploratory
light-ray, we shall have what Heidegger calls *die Lichtung*, the "clearing," in which truth is *experienced*, not
perceived, as part and parcel of the "facticity" (*Tatsächlichkeit*) and historicity (*Geschichtlichkeit*) of man's existence. We must labor not only to reach this clearing
but to dwell in it.

Again and again, the drive—toward objective contemplation, logical analysis, scientific classification, which
cuts us off from being—presses on the Western intellect.
Even Augustine, even the later Luther, even Kierkegaard
the master psychologist succumb to it. This conceptual-
izing impetus edges them away from the genuinely ontological to the merely theoretical, from immersion in being
to a technical diagnosis of the concept of existence. Thus
in all metaphysics as we have known it since Parmenides,
and even in the most existentially biased of philosophic
theologies, "to think" is, in essence, "to see," "to observe."
As a result, *Sein* is something "made present to the eye"
(*Vor-Augen-Sein*). As such, it has remained "unthought,"
Ungedacht, and has not been made articulate in language. This is why Heidegger must begin all over again.

Sein und Zeit will try "to think and say being and Being." It will *try to*. The imperative is, strictly, one of attempt. Heidegger knows this, and says it over and over again. *"Auf einer Stern zugehen, nur dieses"* ("to proceed toward a star, only this"). *"Alles ist Weg"* ("all is way" or "under-wayness," as in the word *tao*). The proceedings of *Sein und Zeit* are *"ein kaum vernehmbares Versprechen"* ("a scarcely audible promise," where, in German, *Versprechen* signifies both "promise" and "error of speech"). The argument is now opaque and confusing, now lit as by a lightning bolt (an image taken from Heraclitus). But how could it be otherwise, when Heidegger is posing the *one* and only question, when he is asking and inviting us to ask, for the first time since the pre-Socratics: *tí tò on*— "What is being, what is beingness in its Being?" *Was ist das Seiende, das Seiende in seinem Sein?* And what is *die Zeit,* that "time" which Western metaphysics has forgotten in the process of abstracting and idealizing being? The title, *Sein und Zeit,* tells us that the two questions are, finally, the same.

To "think Being" is the task of Heidegger's *Fundamentalontologie,* that "ontology of the foundations" which is to be distinguished utterly from the Platonic model of ideal Forms, from the Aristotelian-Aquinian network of cause and substance, from Cartesian scientific rationality, and from Nietzsche's inspired but nihilistic identification of being and will. The "fundamental ontology" is to replace all particular ontologies such as those of "history," of the physical or biological sciences, of sociology. (How, challenges Heidegger, can there be a particular doctrine or method of understanding if there is not, first and foremost, a general grasp of being; what are the methodologies of the distinct sciences and disciplines other than an artifice or evasion of the underlying question?) How does a fundamental ontology proceed? By differentiating absolutely between the "ontic" and the "ontological," that is to say between the realm of external particulars, of beings, and that of Being itself. Let us note at once: the "ontic" and the "ontological" are as different as any two concepts or spheres of reference can be. But the one makes no sense whatever without the other. Think of the reciprocally defining and enabling notions of "day" and "night." There is no "being" without "Being." Without the "beings" whose "isness" it is, "Being" would be as empty a formulation as pure Platonic Form or Aristotle's motionless mover. Only by keeping this distinction sharply in mind can we ask: *Was ist das Seiende in seinem Sein?* In the *Sophist*, Plato equates this question with the attempt of mortals to wrestle with Titans. And we know that even to ask it means a break with constraints of logic and language that have, over two millennia, reduced *ist* to a spectral convention of grammar, to a copula present in all propositions but, existentially, vacant. So, like Heidegger himself, we *try* to ask.

We do. This is Heidegger's methodological starting point. He does not question objects or ideas or logical-grammatical relations. Like Husserl before him, he turns completely to man. For amid all essents, amid all that is and makes up the "ontic" aggregate (*das Seiende*), one being, one *Seiendes*, is manifestly privileged. It is man. And his privilege consists precisely in the fact that he alone experiences existence as problematic, that he alone is an ontic presence seeking a relation of understanding to the ontological, to "Being" itself. This relation Heidegger terms a *Seinsverständnis*. Only man can question Being, can endeavor to "think being" and voice this thought process. But "can" is much too feeble a word. He *must* do so. This is the first and fundamental assertion of *Sein und Zeit*. The actual existence of man, his "human being," depends immediately and constantly on a questioning of Being. This questioning generates and alone makes substantive and significant what Heidegger calls *Existenz*. There is no such thing as an assured, a priori essence of man (Sartre will make this the cardinal point of his teaching). Man achieves his essence, his humanity, in the process of "existence," and he does so by questioning Being, by making his own particular "extantness" questionable. And it is this putting in question which, alone, makes man *fragwürdig,* "deserving of question."

A being that questions Being by first questioning its own *Sein* is a *Da-Sein*. Man is man because he is a "being-there," an "is-there" (English will not weld the requisite amalgam). The *ontic* achieves *Da-Sein* by querying the ontological. It does so, uniquely and necessarily, by means of language. Thus, in a way which only the later Heidegger develops, *Da-Sein* and *Sprache* are mutually determinant. To question *Sein* is to question its *Sinn* —its "sense," its "meaning," its "purpose." Such inquiry may begin "preontologically": by way of biological, psychological, sociological, historical analyses. The results will be "ontic explanations" or an "existential analytic." But if the questioning is real, as in the final analysis neither Kant's nor Husserl's nor Sartre's is, it will always strive toward a "fundamental ontology." It will ask the meaning of Being as such (*der Sinn vom Sein überhaupt*). This is to enter the famous hermeneutic circle. *Da-Sein* must walk this circle and penetrate, through its spiraling inwardness, to the "clearing" where truth becomes "unconcealment."

Man's being must be a "being-there." Heidegger now expounds on the nature of "thereness." The crux is *Alltäglichkeit,* signifying "everydayness." All Western metaphysics, whether deliberately or not, has been Platonist in that it has sought to transpose the essence of man out of daily life. It has posited a pure perceiver, a fictive agent of cognition detached from common experience. It has disincarnated being through an artifice of introspective reductionism of the sort dramatized in Cartesian doubt and Husserlian phenomenology. This is why metaphysics has loftily relinquished the study of perception to psychology, the understanding of behavior to morals or sociology, the analysis of the human condition to the political and historical sciences. Heidegger utterly rejects this process of abstraction and what he regards as the resultant artifice of compartmentalization in man's consideration of men.

Dasein is "to be there" (*da-sein*), and "there" is the world: the concrete, literal, actual, daily world. To be human is to be immersed, implanted, rooted in the earth, in the quotidian matter-of-factness of the world ("human" has in it *humus,* the Latin for "earth"). A philosophy that abstracts, that seeks to elevate itself above the everydayness of the everyday, is empty. It can tell us nothing of the meaning of being, of where and what *Dasein* is. The world *is*—a fact that is, of course, the primal wonder and source of all ontological asking. It is here and now and everywhere around us. We are in it. Totally. (How could we be anywhere "else"?) To express this radical immanence, this embeddedness, Heidegger uses the composite *In-der-welt-sein* (a "being-in-the-world," a "to-be-in-the-world"). Already Husserl, in his emphasis on the concreteness of the human encapsulation in reality, had spoken of a *Lebenswelt,* a "life-world." But Heidegger's "grounding," to use the verb as we do when we speak of "grounding" an electric conductor, is more absolute. *In-Sein,* this "being in," is not the accidental location of water in a glass, of a table in a room. Applied to man's *Dasein,* it is the total determinant of his "being-at-all." There is nothing spiritual or metaphorical about this:

> Hence being-in is not to be explained ontologically by some ontical characterization, as if one were to say, for

instance, that being-in a world is a spiritual property, and that man's "spatiality" is a result of his bodily nature (which, at the same time, always gets founded upon corporeality). Here again we are faced with the being-present-at-hand-together of some such spiritual Thing with a corporeal Thing, while the Being of the entity thus compounded remains more obscure than ever. Not until we understand being-in-the-world as an essential structure of *Dasein* can we have any insight into Dasein's *existential spatiality*. Such an insight will keep us from failing to see this structure or from previously cancelling it out—a procedure motivated not ontologically but rather "metaphorically" by the naïve supposition that man is, in the first instance, a spiritual Thing which subsequently gets misplaced "into" a space.

This supposition, and the mind-body dualism that goes with it, may be "naïve," but it is in fact that of Platonic, Cartesian, and Kantian epistemologies. Heidegger's "mundanity," to use this eroded word in its strongest etymological sense, would overthrow the whole metaphysical mind-body tandem and the dissociation between essential being and being here-and-now. For Heidegger, being-in is not an attribute, it is not an accidental property of extension, as it would be in the Aristotelian idiom:

> It is not the case that man "is" and then has, by way of an extra, a relationship-of-being toward the "world"— a world with which he provides himself occasionally. *Dasein* is never "proximally" an entity which is, so to speak, free from Being-in, but which sometimes has the inclination to take up a "relationship" toward the world. Taking up relationships toward the world is possible only *because Dasein*, as Being-in-the-world, is as it is. This state of Being does not arise just because some other entity is present-at-hand outside of *Dasein* and meets up with it. Such an entity can "meet up with" *Dasein* only insofar as it can, of its own accord, show itself within a *world*.

Heidegger is saying that the notion of existential identity and that of world are completely wedded. To be at all is to be *worldly*. The everyday is the enveloping wholeness of being. The "meeting up" of *Dasein* and the world, which gives definition to both, comes under the humble but immensely important headings of *Tatsächlichkeit* and *Faktizität*. English "facticity" covers only thinly and awkwardly the vehement concreteness of the two terms. We overlook the all-determining centrality of our being-in-the-world because the everyday actualities of this inhabiting are so various and seemingly banal. They consist, says Heidegger, of having to do with something, producing something, attending to and looking after something, making use of something, giving up something and letting it go, undertaking, accomplishing, evincing, interrogating, considering, discussing, determining, and knowing something. This last way of being-in-the-world is especially noteworthy.

Knowing, affirms Heidegger, who is here forcing phenomenology to its limits, is "a mode of being of *Dasein* as being-in-the-world." *Knowing is a kind of being.* Knowledge is not some mysterious leap from subject to object and back again. "The perceiving of what is known is not a process of returning with one's booty to the 'cabinet' of consciousness" (observe how Heidegger fixes on the aggressive, exploitative strain in the classical model of the acquisition of knowledge). It is, on the contrary, a form of being-with, a *concern* (a concept that will be detailed later on) with and inside the world. Where no production, manipulation, or putting to profitable use is intended, such concern is a "tarrying alongside" (*ein Verweilen-bei*). Disinterestedness is, therefore, the highest mode of concern. But, whether disinterestedly or not, to know something is a concrete form of being-in-the-world. This leads Heidegger to a haunting, strangely Platonic correlate: "Even the forgetting of something, in which every relationship of being toward what one formerly knew has been obliterated, must be conceived as a *modification of the primordial being-in;* and this holds for every delusion and for every error." But even as knowledge does not create the world, nor forgetting obliterate it (propositions in which Heidegger is, massively, on the side of common sense), so it must follow that *Dasein* only discovers itself as it grasps reality. What are the main categories of such grasping? (*Begriff*, meaning "concept," is built on *Griff*, the literal, manual grasp of something.) Heidegger calls these categories *Existenzialien.*

This opens the exposition of Heideggerian "anthropology," the famous sections of *Sein und Zeit* in which Heidegger sets out the principal modalities of man's inherence in the world. Much of what Heidegger says is simultaneously obvious and arcane. In order to clarify and, at the same time, to make problematic—and therefore salient—the existential fabric of everyday experience, the seamless texture of being which metaphysics has idealized or scorned, Heidegger welds language into a kind of violent ordinariness. He twists and compacts the sinews of vocabulary and grammar into resistant, palpable nodes. The resultant "antirhetoric" is both highly technical and brutally innocent. As are Expressionist canvases or action-paintings, with their thick swirls and stabs of pigment. The analogy here is a genuine one. Heidegger is striving to get language and his reader inside the actual world, he is trying to make luminous and self-revealing the obstinate opaqueness of matter. Van Gogh can do just this. By some mystery of uttermost concreteness, he reveals to us the complete being-in-the-world, the complete significance of the being-in-the-world of a chair, of a pair of shoes. A total openness to the integral verity of these things "comes out of"—we don't really know *how* —the often violent brushstroke or application of the palette knife. So it is in *Sein und Zeit*. Heidegger's discourse tends to clot, as does thick paint. To read it with any degree of penetration is to sense the dynamics, the roughage of a process rather than its logic or finish. But where one takes "entities as entities within-the-world for one's ontological foothold," the whole point is one of grip.

We are "thrown" (*geworfen*) into the world, proclaims Heidegger. Our being-in-the-world is a "thrownness," a *Geworfenheit*. There is nothing mystical or metaphysical about this proposition. It is a primordial banality which metaphysical speculation has long overlooked. The world into which we are thrown, without personal choice, with no previous knowledge (*pace* Plato), was there before us and will be there after us. Our *Dasein* is inseparable from it and, as we shall see, there is a sense in which the world derives meaning from our *Dasein*. But the relationship is not causal; it is not, as in certain rigorously idealistic models, our awareness that constructs the world. Heidegger's formulation is so awkward as to invite parody or outright refusal, but it is vital to his case:

> This characteristic of *Dasein*'s being—this "that it is"— is veiled in its "whence" and "whither," yet is disclosed in itself the more unveiledly. We call it the *"thrownness"* of this entity into its "there." Indeed, it is thrown in such a way that, as being-in-the-world, it is "there." The expression "thrownness" is meant to suggest the *facticity of its being delivered over*.

Let us attempt to rephrase Heidegger's definition. We certainly do not know whence we came into being, except in the most trivially physiological regard. No biology of parentage answers the real question. We do not know toward what end we have been projected into existence, except in reference to death (whose meaning and ontological status Heidegger has yet to elucidate). Yet it is just this twofold unknowing which makes the "thrown" condition of human existence the more emphatic and palpable. We are "delivered over"—a lame rendition of Heidegger's *Überantwortung*, with its clear connotations of "responsibility toward that into which we are delivered"—to an actuality, to a "there," to a complete, enveloping presentness. *Dasein* must take up this presentness, it must assume it into its own existence. It cannot do otherwise and continue to be. The term *Faktizität* is meant to make unmistakable the imperative "thereness" of the world into which we find ourselves thrown.

It follows that the Cartesian *cogito ergo sum* is a piece of anthropomorphic and rationalistic hyperbole. The reverse is the case: "I am, therefore I think." Existence is the necessary precedent and enabling condition of thought. There is, certainly in the very sense in which Descartes sought to establish the two terms, existence before thought. Thought is only one of the articulations of *Dasein*. Platonic-Cartesian cogitation and the Cartesian foundation of the world's reality in human reflection are attempts to "leap through or across the world" (*ein Überspringen*) in order to arrive at the noncontingent purity of eternal Ideas or of mathematical functions and certitudes. But this attempted leap from and to abstraction is radically false to the facticity of the world as we encounter it, as we live it. How, then, does the world in fact (a turn of phrase which, here, resumes its original strength) meet up with us?

The world comes at us, answers Heidegger, in the form and manner of *things*. But of the obviously innumerable object-entities that *Dasein* encounters, those that will constitute *its* being-in-the-world are not just any things. They are what the Greeks called *pragmata*, "that is to say, that which one has to do with in one's concernful dealings." Heidegger's word for *pragmata* is *Zeug*. It, at times, has been translated as "equipment," "instrumentation," *outillage*. Its principal German derivative is *Werkzeug*, meaning "tool." The distinction between "anything" and *Zeug* is essential to Heidegger's entire world-view. *Vorhandenheit*, which signifies "presentness-at-hand," is the character of the object "out there." It characterizes the matter of theoretic speculation, of scientific study. Thus "Nature" is *vorhanden* to the physicist and rocks are *vorhanden* to the geologist. But this is not how a stonemason or a sculptor meets up with a rock. *His* relationship to stone, the relationship crucial to his *Dasein*, is that of *Zuhandenheit*, of a "readiness-*to*-hand" (observe the formidable gap which separates *at* from *to* in the two instrumental terms). That which is *zuhanden*, literally "to-hand," reveals itself to *Dasein*, is taken up by and into *Dasein*, in ways absolutely constitutive of the "thereness" into which our existence has been thrown and in which it must accomplish its being. Heidegger's account of the "to-handness" of human experience is so dense and tangible that a brief quotation gives only an inadequate feel:

> The process of hammering does not simply have knowledge about (*um*) the hammer's character as a tool, but it has appropriated this tool in a way which could not possibly be more suitable. In dealings such as this, where something is put to use, our concern subordinates itself to the "in-order-to" which is constitutive for the tool we are employing at the time. The less we just stare at the hammer-Thing, and the more we seize hold of it and use it, the more primordial does our relationship to it become, and the more unveiledly is it encountered as that which it is—as tool (*Zeug, Werkzeug*). . . . No matter how sharply we just *look* at the "outward appearance" of Things, in whatever form this appearance takes, we cannot discover anything ready-to-hand (*zuhanden*). If we look at Things just "theoretically,"

we can get along without understanding readiness-to-hand. But when we deal with them by using them and manipulating them, this activity is not a blind one. It has its own kind of sight, by which our manipulation is guided and from which it acquires its own Thingly character.

Appropriate use, performance, manual action *possess their own kind of sight.* Heidegger names it "circumspection." Any artist, any craftsman, any sportsman wielding the instruments of his passion will know exactly what Heidegger means and will know how often the trained hand "sees" quicker and more delicately than eye and brain. Theoretical vision, on the other hand, looks at or upon things noncircumspectively: "It constructs a canon for itself in the form of *method.*" This is the way of the physicist "looking" at atomic particles. Here methodological abstraction replaces the immediate authority of "readiness-to-hand." Heidegger's differentiation is not only eloquent in itself; it brilliantly inverts the Platonic order of values which sets the theoretical contemplator high above the artist, the craftsman, the manual worker.

To speak of work tools is, necessarily, to infer the existence of "others," of those for whom the work is destined. In Part I of *Sein und Zeit* (IV, 26), we find the outlines of what Heidegger would regard as an ontological approach to social theory. The "I" is never alone in its experience of *Dasein.* When "others" are met with, it is not the case that "one's subject is proximally present-at-hand." We encounter others "from out of the *world,* in which concernfully circumspective *Dasein* essentially dwells." The meeting with others is not a contingent, ancillary attribute of subjectivity; it is an essential, integral element in the reciprocal realizations of being and of world. The determinant way in which we come up against *l'autre,* moreover, is "at work." (Here there are genuine points of accord between Heidegger and the Marxist model of the primarily social and collaboratively functional character of the process of human individuation.) "Even if we see the other 'just standing around,' he is never apprehended as a human-Thing present-at-hand. His 'standing around' is an existential mode of being— an unconcerned, uncircumspective tarrying alongside everything and nothing. The other is encountered in his *Dasein* with and in the world." Again the notion of "thrownness" is important. The world into which our *Dasein* is thrown and on which it enters has others in it. The "world's worldhood" is such that the existence of others is absolutely essential to its facticity, to its "being-there" at all. And our grasp of this primordial fact is not arrived at by chance acquaintance or theoretical investigation. Our understanding of the ontological status of others, and of the relationship of such status to our own *Dasein,* is itself a form of being. To understand the presentness of others is to exist. Being-in-the-world, says Heidegger, is a being-with. In stressing this principle, Heidegger is seeking to resolve or identify as "purely metaphysical" the famous problem of how we perceive the existence of other minds, an issue notoriously elusive in Husserl's often solipsistic scheme of personal cognizance.

But being-with also has its negative components. Heidegger's account of these is one of the most penetrating achievements in his whole work. If this account does not actually initiate what was to become a dominant motif in modern sensibility—Durkheim and Engels had preceded *Sein und Zeit*—it nevertheless gives to this motif an unsurpassed incisiveness and reach.

Thrown among others, enacting and realizing our own *Dasein* as an everyday being-with-one-another (Heidegger's ponderous hyphenation images the meshed density of the facts), *we come not to be ourselves*. We come to exist not in and on our own terms, but in reference to, in respect of others—and it is here that the word "others" takes on the coercive coloration of Sartre's *l'autre*. In a completely literal, concrete sense, "we are not ourselves," which is to say that our being is made factitious. Heidegger's key word is lapidary and awkward to translate: the self is alienated from itself and becomes a *Man*. In German, *Mann* signifies both "one" and "they"; only context, and even context not invariably, can resolve this crucial indeterminacy. This *Man*, which we can best render by "oneness" and "theyness" simultaneously, dramatizes the recession of true *Dasein* into alienation, averageness, distance from authentic being, "publicness," and irresponsibility. "Everyone is the other, and no one is himself. The '*they*,' which supplies the answer to the question of the '*who*' of everyday *Dasein*, is the '*nobody*' to whom every *Dasein* has already surrendered itself in being-among-one-another." The being that *is* us is eroded into commonalty; it subsides to a "oneness" within and among a collective, public, herdlike "theyness." Which "theyness" is the aggregate not of veritable beings, but of "ones." We do not yield up the ontological integrity of our *Dasein* into this or that specific keeping, we do not obey a meaningful summons (modes of self-surrender which Heidegger prizes). We yield our existence to a formless "Theyness" or *alterité*. The others to whom we consign ourselves are not definite, sovereign presences: "On the contrary, any other can represent them. What is decisive is just that inconspicuous domination by others which has already been taken over unawares from *Dasein* as being-with."

Heidegger's portrayal of self-estrangement carries intense conviction: "One belongs to the others oneself and enhances their power. The 'others,' whom one thus designates in order to cover up the fact of one's belonging to them essentially oneself, are those who proximally and for the most part '*are there*' in everyday being-with-one-another. The 'who' is not this one, not that one, not oneself, not some people, and not the sum of them all. The 'who' is the neuter, *the 'they.'* " Heidegger's diagnosis relates, to be sure, to Engels' perception of the dehumanization of the individual in a mass society and to Durkheim's analyses of *anomie,* both of which, in turn, point back to the Rousseauist and Hegelian concepts of alienation. But what Heidegger has to say possesses a particular moral-psychological bite and prophetic shrewdness. Distance from being, averageness, the leveling downward of sentiment and expression in a consumer society "constitute what we know as 'publicness.' Every kind of spiritual priority is smoothly suppressed. Overnight, everything that is primordial gets glossed over as something that has long been well known. . . . Every secret loses its force."

A drastic irresponsibility—literally "nonanswerability to"—ensues. And again, Heidegger acutely analyzes the dialectical feedback involved: "Because the 'they' presents every judgment and decision as its own, it deprives the particular *Dasein* of its answerability. The 'they' can, as it were, manage to have 'them' constantly invoking it. It can be answerable for everything most easily, because it is not someone who needs to vouch for anything. It 'was' always the 'they' who did it, and yet it can be said that it has been 'no one.' " Written in, or rather published in, 1927, these observations remain among the deepest, most unsparing that we have on the behavior of the "they" under totalitarianism. But passivity in the face of, or active support for, political barbarism is merely an extension of the everyday. The alienated self, the *Man,* is fatally disburdened of moral autonomy and, therefore, of moral responsibility. It can know no ethical guilt. The self of everyday *Dasein,* in short, "is the *they-self"* (*Das Man-selbst,* an ominous hybrid). It is the very opposite of *Eigentlichkeit,* of the concrete singularity and realness of a *Dasein* which has grasped, which has taken a hold of itself (*eines eigens ergriffenen Selbst*). The distinction is one of the most decisive in Heideggerian thought and in the impact of that thought on modern feeling. It is the distinction between an authentic and an inauthentic condition of human life.

Heidegger now proceeds to actualize and deepen this capital duality. Inauthentic *Dasein* lives not as itself but as "they" live. Strictly considered, it scarcely lives at all. It "is lived" in a hollow scaffolding of imposed, anonymous values. In inauthentic existence we are constantly afraid (of other men's opinions, of what "they" will decide for us, of not coming up to the standards of material or psychological success though we ourselves have done nothing to establish or even verify such standards). Fear of this order is *Furcht.* It is part of the banal, pre-fabricated flux of collective sentiment. *Angst* is radically different. In its Augustinian, Pascalian, and, above all, Kierkegaardian sense, *Angst* is that which makes problematic, which makes worthy of questioning, our being-in-the-world. *Angst* is one of the primary instruments through which the ontic character and context of everyday existence is made inescapably aware of, is rendered naked to, the pressures of the ontological (of which death is, as we shall see, privileged). *Angst* is a mark of authenticity, of the repudiation of "theyness."

Another differentiation follows. We have seen that *Dasein* is grounded in language, that the intelligibility of being-in-the-world expresses itself and can only express itself in discourse. We live, says Heidegger, "by *putting into words* the totality-of-significations of intelligibility. To significations, words accrue." Authentic language is

Rede, a word which, as Heidegger's translators ruefully point out, is often less formal than "discourse," but certainly less colloquial than "talk." In the phenomenality of the everyday, of the "oneness" and the "theyness," *Dasein*'s understanding and self-interpretation come to pass not in *Rede,* but in *Gerede.* Once more, translation is lamed. "Idle talk," "chatter," carry moralistic valuations, which Heidegger wants to avoid precisely because they are themselves far too conventional and comforting for what it is he has to say. Perhaps the best we can do is to think of *Rede* as "speech," as "the speech of *Dasein*"—the association with *logos* lies near to hand—and of *Gerede* as, quite simply, "talk."

This latter heading has a corrosive ubiquity. It embraces not only the floodtide of trivia and gossip, of novelty and cliché, of jargon and spurious grandiloquence "but spreads to what we write, where it takes the form of 'scribbling.'" Overwhelmingly, "talk" has lost "its primary relationship-of-being toward the entity talked about, or else has never achieved such a relationship" (a devastating anatomy of journalism and the idiom of the media). Thus it cannot communicate "in such a way as to let this entity be appropriate in a primordial manner." All that "talk" does is to "pass the word along"—a phrase of forceful contempt as, in German, *Nachreden* also means to asperse, to gossip pejoratively and emptily. *Gerede,* the "one" talking to or, rather, with the "they," is at once the symptom and realization of the rootlessness and restlessness that govern a culture of inauthenticity. "Talk" makes public what should be private. It fosters illusion of understanding without genuine grasp. It obscures or holds back critical inquiry. *Dasein*-with-others transpires in an echo chamber of incessant, vacant loquacity, of pseudocommunication that knows nothing of its cognates which are, or ought to be, "communion" and "community." It is exactly this model that Sartre spells out in *No Exit.*

The fruit of *Gerede* is an obsessive *Neugier,* meaning "curiosity," "lust for novelty":

> Idle talk discloses to *Dasein* a being toward its world, toward others, and toward itself—a being in which these are understood, but in a mode of groundless floating. Curiosity discloses everything and anything, yet in such a way that being-in is everywhere and nowhere. Ambiguity hides nothing from *Dasein*'s understanding, but only in order that being-in-the-world should be suppressed in this uprooted "everywhere and nowhere."

This analysis entails a contrastive ideal of authentic speech, which Heidegger will adduce in his later work, via the great poets. But there is here as well, I think, the apologia, very possibly unconscious, of a man who is writing *Sein und Zeit;* who is contracting, kneading language into novel, recalcitrant shape in order to scour from it the legacy of metaphysical-academic and academic-journalistic chatter. Hence the reiterated, primordial distinction which underlies the entire argument. "Curiosity has nothing to do with observing entities and marveling at them. Curiosity, in this authentic sense, is wonder (*thaumazein*)." Philosophy, which springs from *Neugier,* is (loosely) anchored in "talk." Thought, as Heidegger seeks to exemplify it, is profoundly, almost violently rooted in "the word," whose own wellspring is wonder.

Now there occurs a startling modulation. Heidegger has been differentiating between the authentic and the inauthentic life in terms whose resonance is almost emphatically theological. Heuristic *Angst* has been set against mundane fear; "speech," implying *logos,* has been contrasted with "talk"; the hunger for mere novelty has been opposed to genuine wonder. Each of these opposing rubrics is a natural consequence of the comprehensive antithesis between true *Dasein,* which is self-possession, and the collective indiscrimination of an existence conducted in terms of "oneness" and "theyness." To this latter, Heidegger gives the name *Verfall* ("a falling away from," "a cadence into decline"). Again and pre-eminently, the tonality is theological. It was as if Heidegger's whole diagnosis of inauthenticity amounted to a quasi-secular version of the doctrine of fallen man.

But this, contends Heidegger, is precisely what it is *not.* Inauthenticity and "the falling of *Dasein*" into inauthenticity must *not* be understood as in any way analogous to the scenario of original sin. *Verfall,* says Heidegger, does *not* comport a moral value judgment. Heidegger's explanation of this apparent paradox is not easy to penetrate but must be quoted in full:

> *Dasein* has, in the first instance, fallen away from itself as an authentic potentiality for being its own self. It has fallen into the "world." "Fallenness" into the "world" means an absorption in being-with-one-another, insofar as the latter is guided by idle talk, hunger for novelty and ambiguity. . . . On no account, however, do the terms "inauthentic" and "nonauthentic" signify "really not," as if in this mode of existence *Dasein* were altogether to lose its being. "Inauthenticity" does not mean anything like being-no-longer-in-the-world but amounts rather to a quite distinctive kind of being-in-the-world. This kind is completely fascinated by the "world" and by the *Dasein*-with of others in the "they." Not-being-its-self functions as a *positive* possibility of that entity which, in its essential concern, is absorbed in a world. This kind of *not-being* has to be conceived of as that kind of being which is closest to *Dasein,* and in which *Dasein* maintains itself for the most part.

In other words: because *Dasein* is *always* *Dasein*-with and a being-in-the-world into which we have been thrown, "inauthenticity" and "fallenness" are not accidents or false choices. They are the necessary components of existence, of the existential facticity of the everyday. Being-in-the-world "is itself *tempting*." To accede to the temptation of mundanity is, quite simply, to exist. "Falling" is, therefore, "existentially determinative." How, indeed, could one "fall out of the world"? *Verfall* is a positive in that it makes manifest "an *essential* ontological structure of *Dasein* itself. Far from determining its nocturnal side, it constitutes all *Dasein's* days in their everydayness."

This bold antinomy, this view of the "positivity" of alienation, sets Martin Heidegger's thought sharply apart from that of the two other great models of man's fall in modern Western culture: the Marxist and the therapeutic. The "fallenness" of *Dasein* is not a lapse from some golden age of economic parity and social justice, such as Marx invokes in his more utopian writings. It is not a *Verfall* "from a purer and higher 'primal status.' Not only do we lack any experience of this ontically, but we lack any possibilities or clues for interpreting it." If social reform or revolution will not eliminate inauthenticity, nor will therapy and psychological amendments of personality. Heidegger has no room for any Freudian scenario of original crime and complex. "Fallenness" is the inevitable quality which characterizes an individual's involvement with others and with the phenomenal world. There can be no cure from being.

But "fallenness" is positive in another, deeper sense. There must be inauthenticity and "theyness," "talk" and *Neugier,* so that *Dasein,* thus made aware of its loss of self, *can strive to return to authentic being.* At no point in his work is Heidegger more dialectical, more intent on the dynamics of an argument which springs from internal contradiction. *Verfall* becomes the absolutely necessary precondition for that struggle toward true *Dasein,* toward possession or, rather, repossession of self, which defines man's exposure to the challenge of the ontological. And *pace* Heidegger's denial, the theological model is, at this juncture, obvious and imperative. The "positivity of fallenness" in Heidegger's analysis is an exact counterpart to the celebrated *felix culpa* paradox, to the doctrine which sees in Adam's "happy fall" the necessary precondition for Christ's ministry and man's ultimate resurrection. Via the inauthenticity of its being-in-the-world, *Dasein* is compelled to search out the authentic. Heidegger's postulate is concise but charged with consequence: "authentic existence is not something which floats above falling everydayness. Existentially, it is only a modified way in which such everydayness is seized upon."

What, then, is the proper instrument for this "seizure"? What is the organic relation between the necessary inauthenticity of being-in-the-world and the equally necessary striving for authentic *Dasein*? The answer, given in the last chapter of the first part of *Sein und Zeit*, is *Sorge*.

This arch-Kierkegaardian term is translated by "care," "concern," "apprehension." Heidegger invests it with great positive value and range. In the necessary condition of inauthenticity, we "fall away from ourselves." The phenomenology of the everyday that results from this cadence is one of frenetic inertia. (These two notions are only seemingly contradictory.) In this "innocuous emptiness of a worldless occurring"—Heidegger's phrasing is rebarbative, but his analysis of a simultaneous frenetic busyness and emptiness is acutely telling—there arises from within us a sense of the uncanny. We feel literally *unheimlich*, "homeless," "unhoused." As we flail about emptily, the familiarity of the everyday shatters. It is as if we had been caught, all of a sudden, in the interstices of the busy mesh of being, and stood face to face with the ontological, with the *Daseinsfrage*. It is striking how closely Heidegger's evocation of the uncanny resembles Freud's famous use of the term.

Uncanniness declares those key moments in which *Angst* brings *Dasein* face to face with its terrible freedom to be or not to be, to dwell in inauthenticity or strive for self-possession. In these moments, man knows himself to be "available," "free for" (in *The Flies*, Sartre's dramatization of this vertigo of potentiality, these words are rendered by *disponibilité* and *liberté*). Under stress of the uncanny, *Dasein* comes to realize that beyond being *Dasein*-with and *Dasein*-in—which are the ineluctable modes of the everyday—it must become *Dasein*-for. *Sorge*, signifying "care-for," "concern-for and -with," is the means of this transcendence. It can and must take myriad forms: care for the ready-to-hand, for the tools and materials of our practice; a concern for others which can be defined as "solicitude." But principally, and in a sense yet to be expounded, *Sorge* is a concern with, a caring for, an answerability to, the presentness and mystery of Being itself, of Being as it transfigures beings. And it is from this existential ethic of concernedness that derives Heidegger's subsequent definition of man as the shepherd and custodian of Being.

Now we can grasp the seminal links between inauthenticity and authenticity, between fallenness and that encounter with the ontological which the uncanny forces on the fallen. Being-in-the-world has lost itself inertly (but absolutely inevitably) in what is at its disposal, in what is merely "there." But this loss generates a fertile dissatisfaction. It opens busy, empty *Dasein* to the vertigo of the uncanny. In its dizziness, *Dasein* hungers and wills beyond itself. Ontologically, says Heidegger, dissatisfaction and desire presuppose the possibility of care:

Care is always concern and solicitude, even if only privatively. In willing, an entity which is understood—that is, one which has been projected upon its possibility—gets seized upon, either as something with which one may concern oneself, or as something which is to be brought into its being through solicitude.

Desire and hope are the reaching-forward of care. Thus care underlies and necessitates "the possibility of *being-free*." The careless man and the uncaring are not free. It is *Sorge* that makes human existence meaningful, that makes a man's life signify. To be-in-the-world in any real, existentially possessed guise, is to care, to be *besorgt* ("careful"). Again, the fundamental equation is anti-Cartesian: I care, therefore I am. The terminology may be contorted and the articulations of argument difficult to test. But the implicit vision is one of vehement humanity, endowed with that somber zest characteristic of Augustine, of Pascal, of Kierkegaard.

Care, concludes Heidegger, is the "primordial state of being" of *Dasein* as it strives toward authenticity. But what of Being itself? What meaning has *Sein*? What is this "Being" of which beings are to have an eminent solicitude and guardianship? To ask this is to start all over again, in a retracing, spiraling motion which is, as we have noted, fundamental to Heidegger's whole method.

We go back to our title: *Being and Time*. Just how do they relate? Part II of *Sein und Zeit* sets out to establish the total interaction, the mutual determination of the two concepts. A fundamental ontology is that in which being is shown to be inseparable from temporality (*Zeitlichkeit*). "Outside time"—a meaningless phrase—existence can have no sense. It can be neither experienced nor thought meaningfully. "Care," which is, as we saw, the existential mode in and through which being grasps its own necessary location and implication in the world, "must use time, and therefore must reckon with time." It is "in time" that essents within-the-world are met with. It is only inside the "horizon of time," a phrase that Heidegger himself felt to be central to his vision but also lastingly problematic, that meaning can be ascribed to ontic realities, to the fabric and contents of the everyday, and to such ontological finalities as "Being in general." Hence the lapidary assertion that "temporality makes up the primordial meaning of *Dasein*'s being."

Again, we note the anti-Platonic and anti-Cartesian slant. In both Plato and Descartes, the determining coordinates of all knowledge are those of geometrical space and of idealized time or eternity. Consciously or not, Heideggerian temporality relates to that framework of individualized, eschatologically differentiated time which is postulated by the fact that the Incarnation takes place *in time*. (The point is made emphatically by Saint Augustine, so often Heidegger's predecessor.) When we contrast Plato's time or Descartes's with that of *Sein und Zeit*, what we are dealing with is nothing less than two radically opposed ways of placing human existence and the meaning of this existence. In the very famous but often misread opening chapters of this second part of the book, Heidegger's eschatological focus becomes graphic.

Dasein can come to grasp its own wholeness and the meaningfulness that is indivisible from integrity only when it faces its "no-longer-being-there" (*sein Nicht-mehr-da-sein*). So long as *Dasein* has not come to its own end, it remains incomplete. It has not completed its *Gänze* ("entirety"). *Dasein* has access to the meaning of being —this is an immensely important point—because and only because that being is finite. Authentic being is therefore a *being-toward death*, a *Sein-zum-Tode* (one of the most often cited, least understood tags in modern thought).

Our first, objective approach to the phenomenon of *Dasein*'s termination which is death comes to pass through the death of others. Because being is always a being-with-others, we literally "gain an experience of death" at numerous moments during our own existence. Moreover, and Heidegger here is at his most strangely poignant, the dying of others confronts us with "that remarkable phenomenon of being which may be defined as the change-over of an entity from *Dasein*'s kind of being (or life) to no-longer-*Dasein*. The *end* of the entity *qua Dasein* is the *beginning* of the same entity *qua* something present-at-hand." The deceased has abandoned our world, but in terms of being, "those who remain can still *be with him*." At one level, Heidegger is reaffirming the constantly participatory, shared quality of existential everydayness, the "being-withness" of all being. At another level, he is adducing the perfectly ordinary but profound psychological truth that the dead can be closer to us, more actively with us, more fully a part of our being, than the living. The study of a dead man's thoughts, the contemplation of his art, the fulfillment of his political purpose, the intense recall of his "thereness," are instances of "care" which are entirely typical of *Dasein*. They show how the death of an individual is very often a modulation toward resurrection in other men's needs and remembrance. Heidegger's term is "respectful solicitude." It provides a clue to the primordial importance which he will attach to the theme of Sophocles's *Antigone* and to the whole question of how a living community must constitute a "being-along-side" its dead.

Nevertheless, however "careful," however vivid our apprehension of the death of others, we cannot experience, we cannot take genuine part in, that coming-to-an-end.

The being-toward-death of each individual is crucial to *Dasein* itself, and it is inalienable. Heidegger's statement (with its seeming echo of Rilke's famous prayer for a "death of one's own") has been formidably influential:

> *No one can take the other's dying away from him.* Of course, someone can "go to his death for another." But this always means to sacrifice oneself for the other "*in some definite affair.*" Such "dying for" can never signify that the other has thus had his death taken away from him in the slightest degree. Dying is something that every *Dasein* itself must take upon itself at the time. By its very essence, death is in every case mine insofar as it "is" at all. And indeed, death signifies a peculiar possibility-of-being in which the very being of one's own *Dasein* is an issue. In dying, it is shown that "mineness" and existence are ontologically constitutive for death. Dying is not an event; it is a phenomenon to be understood existentially.

The inalienability of death—the plain but overwhelming fact that each must die for himself, that death is the one existential potentiality which no enslavement, no promise, no power of "theyness" can take away from individual man—is the fundamental truth of the meaning of being. *Dasein* is always a *not-yet*, an unripeness (the term is precisely that of the great Expressionist metaphysician of hope Ernst Bloch). To be is to be incomplete, unfulfilled. But at the same time, all authentic *being is a being-toward-its-own-end*. "Death is a way to be, which *Dasein* takes upon itself as soon as it is." And Heidegger quotes a medieval homily which instructs us that "as soon as man enters on life, he is at once old enough to die." The essence, the motion, the meaning of life are totally at one with being-toward-death, with the individual's "assumption" (Sartre's derivative, key term) of his own singular death. Thus "death is, in the widest sense, a phenomenon of life"; indeed, it may well be *the* identifying phenomenon, though it cannot itself "be lived" (a point on which Heidegger concurs explicitly with Wittgenstein). The point to be stressed is at once existential and logical: the possibility of *Dasein* depends on and makes sense only in respect of the "impossibility of *Dasein*" which is death. The one cannot *be* without the other.

But precisely inasmuch as death is a reality-in-the-world and concomitant of being, it too can fall into the temptations of inauthenticity. In its felt pressure, Heidegger's account of inauthentic death rivals and may have been influenced by that given by Tolstoi in *The Death of Ivan Ilyich*. "Dying, which is essentially mine in such a way that no one can be my representative, is perverted into an event of public occurrence which the 'they encounters.' " "One dies"—a phrase fatally revelatory of a banalized, existentially spurious, and estranged experience. This alienation is prepared for and buttressed by the rhetoric of medical optimism and social taboo. To think on death is regarded as a sign of morbid insecurity and pathological inadequacy on the part of *Dasein*. The chattering "they" "does not allow us the courage for anxiety in the face of death." (Again, the distinction being made is that between the negative mundanity of "fear" and the ontologically vital "care" that comes of *Angst*. Thus an authentic death has to be striven for. A true being-toward-the-end is one which labors consciously toward fulfillment and refuses inertia; it is one which seeks an ontological grasp of its own finitude rather than taking refuge in the banal conventionality of general biological extinction.

Holding before itself the constant and total possibility of death, a possibility inseparable from its thrownness into the world and process of individualization, *Dasein* "is in anxiety." *Angst* is the taking upon oneself of the nearness of nothingness, of the potential non-being of one's own being. "Being-toward-death is, in essence, anxiety," and those who would rob us of this anxiety—be they priests, physicians, mystics, or rationalist quacks—by transforming it into either fear or genteel indifference alienate us from life itself. Or, more exactly, they insulate us from a fundamental source of freedom. The passage, to which the entire death-and-freedom dialectic of Camus and Sartre is no more than a rhetorical footnote, is a famous one: *Angst* reveals to *Dasein* the possibility of fulfilling itself "in an impassioned FREEDOM TOWARD DEATH—a freedom which has been released from the illusions of the 'they,' and which is factual, certain of itself, and anxious." We can see now that the very meaning of *Dasein* is "in time." Temporality is made concrete by the overwhelming truth that all being is a being-toward-death. The taking upon oneself, through *Angst*, of this existential "terminality" is the absolute condition of human freedom.

This celebrated analysis has often been read as all too typical of Teutonic death-obsessions and portentous fatality. Undoubtedly, there is in Heidegger's argument a dual tradition of pessimism: that of Augustinian-Pascalian-Kierkegaardian insistence on the centrality and utter solitude of individual death, and that of the Romantic identification of death with life's most intense and crowning realization. We find such identification in Keats and, again, in the expressionism of Rilke and, above all, of Trakl. But Heidegger's argument is both technical and positive. The refusal to see death as "an event," the stress on the dialectical oneness of existence and ending, arises closely and consequentially from the whole construct of "being" and of "time," of *Sein* and of *Zeit*. Moreover, Heidegger's emphasis on the inalienability of personal death and on the generative function of *Angst* is profoundly liberating. The notion of *freedom toward death* is no placating addendum, but a rigorously derived lemma, or correlate. As Michael Gelven puts it, in his commentary on *Being and Time*, a genuine view of death "is a bracing awareness of one's finitude." Without finitude there can be no truth. We are at the antipodes to Plato.

The exposition of *Dasein*'s boundenness to death and, *therefore*, to freedom marks the apex of Heidegger's onto-logical "anthropology," of the attempt to ground the nature of being in that of man and man's everyday existence in this world. After this, the deep-breathing intensity of vision, the organic cohesion, seems to go out of *Sein und Zeit*. It is not only that the terminology grows even more opaque and forced but that the sequence of sections and propositions is no longer immediately persuasive.

Sections 54ff spiral back to the earlier considerations on authenticity and "theyness," considerations already given their uttermost extension and logic in the incisive discrimination between authentic and alienated death. Heidegger now reverses his steps in order to show that "theyness" and alienation are not the inevitable fate of *Dasein*-in-the-world, though they are the necessary condition or stage of its "fallenness" and involvement with others. The potential authenticity of *Dasein* is made manifest and, in a sense, guaranteed by a threefold instrumentality of "conscience," of "call" or "summons" (*Ruf*), and of "resoluteness" (*Entschlossenheit*). The "call of conscience" is, literally, inward discourse: "Conscience discourses solely and constantly in the mode of keeping silent."

Its summonses are distinct and immediate. The fact that they are not voided or verbalized does not relegate this phenomenon to "the indefiniteness of a mysterious voice, but merely indicates that our understanding of what is 'called' is not to be tied up with any expectation of anything like a communication (or message)." *Gewissen*, "conscience," is an appeal to the "they-self" to return to being "its-self." It is a silent appeal just because it would compel

Dasein "into the reticence of itself." The summoner is *Dasein* "in its uncanniness: primordial, thrown being-in-the-world as the not-at-home." We experience a primal "guilt" (*Schuld*) at the very fact that the source of our being, the cause of our thrownness, is a nothingness, a *Nichtigkeit*, or, more exactly, that our being necessarily implies the possibility of non-being. Like *Angst*, "guilt" brings us face to face with the ontological question, with the paradoxical challenge that *Dasein* is never, can never be, the origin of its own being, but must take that being upon itself and bring it to its full realization. This confrontation entails choice (again, Heidegger is reiterating an earlier postulate in a somewhat modified form). If there is not a biological sense in which we cannot choose to have been thrown into being, there is an ontological and an ethical sense: one can opt for inauthenticity and "they-ness" even unto death. The summons of conscience, and the state of guilt which this summons induces in *Dasein* —and none of these terms, insists Heidegger, carries any conventionally didactic, homiletic values—press upon us the potentiality of choosing authentically, of realizing against all inertia and mundanity the possibility of "being-for-its-self." Thus the concatenation of "care," "anxiety," and "guilt" is profoundly creative in that it makes choice inescapable.

The attempt to achieve authenticity is expressed by "resoluteness." This is the term which Sartre translates as *engagement,* and which has passed into Anglo-Saxon cultural and political speech as "commitment." For "resoluteness" toward authenticity is not solipsistic; it does not alienate *Dasein* from others. On the contrary: "Resoluteness brings the self right into its current concernful being-alongside what is ready-to-hand, and pushes it into solicitous being with others." Heidegger is arguing that possession of self and rejection of "theyness" do not, as they seem to in Kierkegaard and Nietzsche, cut off the individual from social responsibility. They make him more apt to take such responsibility upon *himself* (a term which, as we have seen, comports a full realization of identity and autonomy). This idea—that *Dasein* can transcend alienation through personal authenticity, that true authenticity entails active involvement with others—will be a seminal notion for Herbert Marcuse and the whole Marxist-Socialist wing of postwar existentialism. Care and genuine "selfhood" are indivisible. Resolutely projecting itself toward its own freely assumed death, and thus toward freedom itself, *Dasein* takes on its personal and its social destiny. But such projection presupposes an ontological understanding of *time*. It is to this that we now turn.

Even by Heideggerian standards, the exposition of the three primary modes, or *Ekstasen,* of temporality is hermetic. At this crucial juncture, the reason may well be that Heidegger had himself not arrived at a satisfactory model of "time-ness" and its determinant interaction with being. The underlying scheme of argument is fairly clear. *Innerzeitigkeit* ("within-timeness") is the vulgar, inauthentic temporality of the everyday, the temporality so largely fixed and imposed on us by "them." But, once again, such inauthenticity is not to be condemned as an evitable weakness or moral flaw. It is the necessary stratum from which *Dasein* must tear itself away in order to reach temporal authenticity and that ontological kinship between being and time which Heidegger expresses in one of the most gnomic of his formulations: *die Zeitigung der Zeit* ("the temporalization, the bringing to maturity of time"). This access to genuine temporality demands a re-evaluation of the banal construct of past-present-future whereby we, almost invariably without giving it thought, imagine and conduct our daily lives. But the revaluation will be one in which this banal triad is preserved and even granted a certain unavoidable legitimacy. At which point, the German language, with its eager vulnerability to etymological torsion, provides Heidegger with invaluable assistance.

Dasein's self-projection toward fulfillment, that motion-toward which is implicit in caring-for, postulates futurity. *"The primary meaning of existentiality is the future."* In German, "future" is *Zukunft,* that "which comes toward one." In seeking to be, *Dasein* is constantly ahead of itself and anticipatory. There is, therefore, a literal sense in which futurity is the most immediate, the most present, of the dimensions of temporality. "To the anticipation which goes with resoluteness, there belongs a present in accordance with which a resolution discloses the situation." Here also, etymology is pressed into service. German "present" is *Gegenwart,* which Heidegger hyphenates as *Gegen-wart* and interprets as meaning "a waiting-toward" or "waiting-against," with "against" signifying, as it still can in Shakespeare and the Authorized Version of the Bible, "in the neighborhood of," "in proximity to." "Present-ness" is "a way of being-alongside." Resoluteness recalls the present from distraction by the object of the everyday and makes of the realized moment an "ecstasy" of "care-ful" anticipation. In authentic temporality, "being-along-side" is also a "waiting-toward that which is coming" (the *Zukünftige*). In *Gewesenheit,* the past or "pastness," Heidegger fixes on the radical *wesen,* "being." This pastness of being is no inert, expended, settled dimension as vulgar usage would have us suppose. *Gewesenheit* is the essential agent of futurity, of that projection toward authentic being which is the existential purpose of *Dasein.* Heidegger's terminology reaches new extremes of impenetrability: "As authentically futural, *Dasein is* authentically as *'having been.'* Anticipation of one's uttermost and ownmost pos-sibility is a coming back, understandingly, to one's ownmost 'been.' Only so far as it is futural can *Dasein be* authentically as having been. The character of 'having been' arises, in a certain way, from the future." "Become what you are," urged Nietzsche.

On the naïve level, Heidegger is expounding the psychological truism that past events are altered and given meaning by what happens now and will happen tomorrow; that the past is rendered either significant or empty by what is yet to be; that it is only a coming to ripeness which gives to what came before a logic and motion. As Coleridge wrote to Charles Aders in 1823: "Without Memory there can be no hope—the Present is a phantom known only by its pining, if it do not breathe the vital air of the Future: and what is the Future, but the Image of the Past projected on the mist of the Unknown, and seen with a glory round its head." Heidegger is reminding us of the mutually generative and reinterpretative circularities of past-present-future. The latent paradox, imaged by the snake eating its own tail or by a Moebius strip, is already familiar to the pre-Socratics. It is a staple of meditation among mystics. The poet tells us that in our end was our beginning. Heidegger's summation comes very close: "only as long as *Dasein* is, *can* it *be* as having been." *Sein* and *Zeit* are as one.

The last part of the book remains a fragment.[1] Having shown that *Dasein* is ineluctably and fundamentally temporal, Heidegger argues that the principal embodiment of this temporality is *history*. But what is "history" really about? How does it relate to individual existence? In what

[1] Commentary on it has been fitful or polemic. The most acute is still Marcuse's 1932 preface to his dissertation on Hegel's ontology and the theory of historicism. Lukács and Adorno have seen in these closing chapters an ominous mystification of the entire issue of historical man and society.

ways is it a structure made up of the three "ecstasies" of timeness?

To elucidate these questions, Heidegger introduces yet another triplet of key terms: *Erbe* ("legacy," "heritage"), *Schicksal* ("fate"), and *Geschick* ("destiny"). Etymology, of course, is at work. In *Schicksal* and *Geschick*, Heidegger hears *schicken*, the verb "to send." Fate is that which has been sent to *Dasein: Geschick* is the "sending" or, as a number of commentators and translators have boldly but accurately proposed, the "mittence." The connections between our words "destiny" and "destination" give a roughly analogous effect. The future, says Heidegger, can only come toward the self insofar as this self is a having-been. Thus the future is meaningful only if it is an *Erbe*, an inheritance, and to the extent that *Dasein* is itself an heir-to. In its inheritance, *Dasein* finds its potentialities, its coming-to-be and being-toward all over again. The crucial process is one of re-petition, of an ontological asking-again.

But whereas "fate" is individual, destiny or "mittence" is collective. It is *Dasein*-in-community. Richardson's paraphrase is scrupulous: in the condition of meaningful temporality which is history, *Dasein* "is not just an isolated unit; its ontological structure includes a with-being with others. Hence the coming-to-pass, structured by historicity, is achieved with other There-beings, all of which constitute a community or a people." An exceedingly important, unmistakably political consequence follows: "the historical There-being cannot achieve its own individual authenticity apart from the community. The heritage which There-being assumes in authenticity, then, is not simply its individual history but somehow the heritage of the entire people *with* which it *is*." To accept one's *Dasein* in the full sense is to enter on one's true historical inheritance. To take one's fate upon oneself is to answer to a mittence of "sending." It is to accept actively one's individual finitude and the need to choose among finite options, but options that involve the community and the individual's afterlife in the destiny of the group. Destiny is fate made authentic on the national or ethnic level. History is not a catalogue of facts; it is not a "free-floating sequence of experiences which 'subjects' have had." It is resoluteness applied to *Dasein*'s heritage; it is the dynamic embedding of individual fate in communal destiny. All the terms, with their portentous and threatening overtones, interlock: *"Only authentic temporality which is at the same time finite makes possible something like fate, that is to say, authentic historicality."*

Sein und Zeit breaks off in midstream. Heidegger closes with a series of unanswered questions. Being was to be explained *aus der Zeit* ("by virtue of," "from within," "in derivation from" time). The third part, which, so far as is known, was never written, was intended to pierce to the final desideratum: an understanding of the meaning of Being, of the *Sinn vom Sein*, as this meaning is determined by the horizon of time. But at the abrupt point of termination, the crucial questions stand naked. How is one to think the transcendence from beings to Being? How is the everyday timeliness of *Dasein* to relate to that authentic temporality which is "the transcendental horizon of the question of Being" (an almost wholly incomprehensible phrase)? What we have in hand is a meandering, self-subverting, often provisional edifice, though on a monumental scale and shot through with inspiration. Key definitions and demonstrations are either postponed or sublimated through tautology. The essential strategy is one of "towardness," of a journey which is only at its start. The grounds of incompletion lay at the heart of Heidegger's undertaking. They were, in decisive respects, to govern both his subsequent works and silences.

In the years immediately after 1927, Heidegger's thought underwent strenuous revision. His *magnum opus* was harvesting fame and influence. But he himself felt that *Sein und Zeit* had, at certain vital points, come to a dead end, that it had not broken out of the prison of metaphysics. Heidegger's analysis now concentrated on two issues, both of which, to be sure, had already figured prominently in his concept of a fundamental ontology. These two issues are "truth" and "language."

Rejecting the Aristotelian-Thomistic and Cartesian view of truth as that of an agreement or adequation between perception and object, Heidegger had already argued in *Sein und Zeit* for a more primordial, authentic definition. He derived it—spuriously, say the scholars—from the Greek word for "truth," *aletheia,* which he translated as "the unconcealed." The truth is that "unhiddenness" which shows, which shines through that which "is true" (whose existence is a truth of being). First delivered as a lecture in 1930, revised in 1940, and published in 1943, *Vom Wesen der Wahrheit* (*On the Essence of Truth*) represents an intense deepening and elaboration of this theme. In *Being and Time,* the emphasis lies on unconcealment and on the fact that man, in his *Dasein,* is the privileged medium in and through which the truth unfolds itself. Now Heidegger modulates toward a more esoteric and non-humanistic view.

In the famous simile of the cave, Plato had made the truth subject to "ideas"; he had equated the truth with "rightness," "correctness," "verifiability" in a strongly positive-scientific sense. This places man at the commanding fulcrum of being. It must lead, as we have seen, to that pragmatic and technological imperialism over knowledge which proceeds via Cartesian rationality to the Nietzschean exaltation of will and modern nihilism. Now, Heidegger begins to give concealment ontological precedence over unconcealment. It is the mark and nature of significant truth to stay hidden, though radiant in and through this occlusion. Man, moreover, is not the enforcer, the opener of truth (as Aristotle, Bacon, or Descartes would have him), but the "opening for it," the "clearing" or *Lichtung* in which it will make its hiddenness manifest. In *What Is Metaphysics?* of 1929, Heidegger advances into even stranger spheres of argument. Truth, he says, relates fundamentally to "nothingness." This "nothingness," however, is not *nihil* ("nothing"), or *Vernichtung* ("annihilation"). It is *Nichtung*, an untranslatable neologism in which "negation" is made an active, creative force. This negation takes away from *Dasein* its self-evidence, its habitual inertia. It restores to *Dasein* its primal astonishment in the face of being. To be thus astonished is to stand before the Pascalian abyss of seminal "nothingness." It is to lay oneself open to the concealed presentness of the truth.

But as he advances these suppositions, Heidegger begins to realize that the incompletions and obscurities of *Sein und Zeit* are not a result of technical, compositional inadequacy. In seeking to overcome metaphysics, Heidegger had, in fact, fallen back into the language of metaphysics, albeit wrenched into idiosyncratic shapes. This language cannot achieve access to the essential *Geheimnis* ("secret," "in-dwelling") of the truth, to that *Verborgenheit* ("hiddenness," "lodgement-within") of generative nothingness at the heart of being. If being is to be thought in depth, if Western thought and society are to be freed from their anthropomorphism, from their arrogant humanism, a new kind of language must be found. Already, Heidegger is moving toward the idea that it is not man who speaks meaningfully, but language itself speaking through man, and through certain poets above all. By 1933, he is turning, increasingly, to Hölderlin. But, of course, events are intruding.

Though voluminous, the literature on Heidegger's involvement with Nazism does not seem to press home the two questions that need asking. What, if anything, relates the fundamental ontology of *Sein und Zeit* to this involvement? What, if anything, can be said to account for Heidegger's *total* public silence (with one jejune posthumous exception) *after* 1945, concerning the holocaust and his own attitudes toward the policies and bestialities of the Third Reich? The restriction to "public" may or may not be relevant; there may or may not be private pronouncements in the archive, for instance in the correspondence with Hannah Arendt.

To wade through the pertinent material is a sickening business. So far as they can be reconstructed, the facts are these:

In April 1933, Professor von Möllendorf, a Social Democrat, is prevented from assuming the rectorship of Freiburg University. He, together with his senior colleagues, asks Heidegger to take on the post. His fame may be of salutary use to the university in threatening times. Heidegger belongs to no party and has taken no role whatever in politics. He hesitates, but is persuaded. Heidegger is elected rector with only one dissenting vote and begins his term of office on April 21. To do so at all is tantamount to becoming a functionary under the new regime, and he joins the National Socialist Party during the first days of May. At the very start of his rectorship Heidegger prohibits the dissemination of anti-Semitic tracts by Nazi students inside the university building. He forbids a planned book-burning of "decadent," "Jewish," and "Bolshevik" works in front of the university, and tries to prevent the purge of "undesirable" volumes from the university library. It is roughly at this point that we come to one of the most notorious items in the entire dossier: Heidegger's alleged authorization of the banning from use of the library of his non-Aryan teacher and predecessor, Edmund Husserl. To the best of my knowledge, no such authorization was issued. If the two men did not see one another in those sick days, the reason was that they had already drifted apart on personal and philosophic grounds. (Heidegger's failure to intervene positively and publicly on Husserl's behalf is, of course, another matter altogether.)

Refusing to ratify the dismissal of two anti-Nazi deans of the university, Wolf and von Möllendorf, Heidegger resigns his rectorship in late February 1934. (It is vital to remember that Hitler assumed complete domination only on August 19, 1934, after the death of Hindenburg.) On resigning, or immediately thereafter, Heidegger leaves the party. Nazi hacks, such as Professor Ernst Krieck, now denounce Heidegger as an obscurantist whose world-view is, despite momentary appearances, the very opposite of the Führer's. There is some evidence that Heidegger's courses, particularly on Nietzsche, are placed under surveillance from the winter semester of 1934–35 onward. A new edition of *Sein und Zeit* appears in 1942. The dedication to Edmund Husserl is omitted. To the best of my knowledge, it is the publisher who insists on this omission, without which the book would not have been allowed. All the laudatory references to Husserl, including the famous footnote on page 38, stand as before. In the summer of 1944, the university authorities declare Heidegger to be "the professor whose services can be most readily dispensed with." As a result, Heidegger is sent to do a spell of compulsory work on the construction of earthworks on the banks of the Rhine. He gives his final class on November 8, 1944. The Allied powers forbid Heidegger to teach. This interdict is in force until 1951.

The key texts for this period are Heidegger's address to colleagues and students on the occasion of the loyalty oath pledged to the new regime in March 1933; his rector's address on the "Self-determination of the German University" in May 1933; his declaration of support for the referendum of November 12, 1933, in which Hitler called on Germany to ratify its exit from the League of Nations; his commemoration, on June 1, 1933, of the death of Albert Leo Schlageter, a nationalist martyr executed by the occupying French forces in the Ruhr; the speech on "Labor-Service and University" of June 20, 1933; and the loosely related "Summons to Labor Battalions" of January 23, 1934. A further document is provided by a photograph of Rector Heidegger surrounded by uniformed Nazi officials and thugs at a celebration of refusal and vengeance on Armistice Day 1933.

As one looks at these texts, and the shorter pronouncements that were made during Heidegger's rectorship, there can be no doubt whatever: it is vile, turgid, and brutal stuff in which the official jargon of the day blends seamlessly with Heidegger's idiom at its most hypnotic. The *Volk* has won back the "truth" of its "will to be," of its *Daseinswillen*. The genius of Adolf Hitler has led his people out of the idolatries and corruptions of "rootless and impotent thinking." It is the National Socialist revolution which will enable philosophers, now reunited to the *Volk* as a whole, to return with "hard clarity" (a characteristic bit of ontological-Nazi idiom) to the question of the meaning of human existence. It is the "supreme privilege" of the academic community to serve the national will. The sole justification for "so-called 'intellectual labor' " is the investment of such labor in the historical, national needs and purposes from which it has sprung. For a university student, to enter the labor battalions of the new Reich is not to waste or betray his calling. On the contrary, it is to give that calling its ethical and social foundations without which, as *Sein und Zeit* has shown, there can be no authentic destiny.

By breaking with the past, by smashing the sham brotherhood of the League of Nations, by yielding itself into "the keeping of the Führer and of that world-historical movement" which he incarnates, Germany is exemplifying, as no other people has ever done, that projection of being toward futurity which is the supreme act of authentication. (The kinship of the vocabulary with that of Part III of *Sein und Seit* is organic.) A plebiscite for Hitler is "a vote for the future"—a future which is the "truer" for being the long-awaited inheritance, the being-past (*Erbe* and *Gewesenheit*) of the German people. "The Führer himself," proclaims Heidegger in the *Freiburger Studenten Zeitung* for November 3, 1933, "is the only present embodiment and future embodiment of German action and its law." To oppose him would be treason against being.

Yet one must note that there are, in the midst of these brutal effronteries and servilities, some covert but tenacious indirections. The address attendant on the loyalty oath speaks of a system that will eschew "the rule of might." The notorious *Rektorats-Rede* has in it hints that the revolution which is being hailed is, or must become, one of spiritual essence rather than politics in the normal sense. The attack on the League of Nations urges the need for a much deeper conception of peace among peoples, for the realization that every nation, not Germany alone, must find for itself the grandeur and the truth of its *Bestimmung* (its "determination," "its assignment through its calling"). Considered closely, a number of key passages dissolve into a curious mist of quietism somewhere to the other side of politics.

Heidegger's *Introduction to Metaphysics* goes back to lectures given in 1935. Heidegger reissues the text in 1953. He retains the following statement: "The works that are being peddled about nowadays as the philosophy of National Socialism but have nothing whatever to do with the inner truth and greatness of this movement [namely the encounter between global technology and modern man] have all been written by men fishing in the troubled waters of 'values' and 'totalities.'" Thus the "inner truth and greatness" of the Nazi movement stands affirmed. As R. Minder has shown, Heidegger's study of Hebbel, *Dichter in der Gesellschaft* (*The Poet in His Society*) of 1966, is replete with Nazi jargon of *Blut und Boden* and the sanctified mission of the *Volk*. On September 23, 1966, Martin Heidegger gave a lengthy interview to the magazine *Der Spiegel* (an oddly trivializing venue) on condition that it appear posthumously. It was published in June 1976. It is masterly in its feline urbanity and evasions. Heidegger acknowledges that he saw no alternative to Nazism in 1933 if Germany were to survive. But before even the crassest of his 1933–34 utterances are to be judged, they must be "thought through" in depth. Where he called for a self-renewal of the German universities under the aegis of the party, it is not the latter that should be emphasized but the ontological connotations of *self*. Compromises in phraseology and public stance were unavoidable if higher education was to be safeguarded. Whatever their unfortunate personal differences, Heidegger continued to draw on Husserl's teachings in his own expositions of phenomenology. The Hölderlin lectures of 1934–35, the Nietzsche seminar of 1936, "spied upon by official informants," ought, in essence, to be seen as an encoded counterstatement to and polemical confrontation with Nazism (*eine Auseinander-*

setzung). What the demure interviewers did not ask was this: Is there anywhere in Heidegger's work a repudiation of Nazism, is there anywhere, from 1945 to his death, a single syllable on the realities and philosophic implications of the world of Auschwitz? These are the questions that count. And the answer would have to be, No.

My own reading of the evidence is this: Like millions of other German men and women, and a good many eminent minds outside Germany, Heidegger was caught up in the electric trance of the National Socialist promise. He saw in it the only hope for a country in the grip of economic and social disaster. The Nazism to which Heidegger adhered, moreover, was, as yet, masking its essential barbarism. It was Heidegger's error and vanity, so characteristic of the academic, to believe that he could influence Nazi ideology, that he could bring his own doctrine of existential futurity to bear on the Hitlerite program, while at the same time preserving the prestige and partial autonomy of the scholarly establishment. He was fatuously mistaken. But if the photograph I have referred to is anything to go by, Heidegger was, already by November 1933, acutely uncomfortable among his Nazi colleagues. His official implication in the movement lasted only nine months and he quit—the point is worth reiterating—before Hitler's assumption of total power. Many eminent intellectuals did far worse.

But the spate of articles and speeches of 1933–34 cries out against Martin Heidegger. For here he goes so crassly beyond official obligation, let alone a provisional endorsement. The evidence is, I think, incontrovertible: there *were* instrumental connections between the language and vision of *Sein und Zeit*, especially the later sections, and those of Nazism. Those who would deny this are blind or mendacious. In both—as in so much of German thought after Nietzsche and Spengler—there is the presumption, at once mesmerized by and acquiescent in, of a nearing apocalypse, of so deep a crisis in human affairs that the norms of personal and institutional morality must be and shall inevitably be brushed aside. There was in the pseudomessianism of the Hitler phenomenon a confirmation of some of Heidegger's most shadowy but deep-seated apprehensions. Both Nazism and the ontological anthropology of *Sein und Zeit* stress the concreteness of man's function in the world, the primordial sanctity of hand and body. Both exalt the mystical kinship between the laborer and his tools in an existential innocence which must be cleansed of the pretensions and illusions of abstract intellect. With this emphasis goes a closely related stress on rootedness, on the intimacies of blood and remembrance that an authentic human being cultivates with his native ground. Heidegger's rhetoric of "at-homeness," of the organic continuum which knits the living to the ancestral dead buried close by, fits effortlessly into the Nazi cult of "blood and soil." Concomitantly, the Hitlerite denunciations of "rootless cosmopolitans," the urban riffraff, and unhoused intelligentsia that live parasitically on the modish surface of society, chime in readily with the Heideggerian critique of "theyness," of technological modernity, of the busy restlessness of the inauthentic.

Heideggerian "resoluteness" (*Entschlossenheit*) has more than a hint of the mystique of commitment, of self-sacrificial and self-projective élan preached by the Führer and his "hard-clear" acolytes. Both enact that heightening of personal fate into national and ethnic vocation which is analyzed in *Sein und Zeit*. In both there is, logically and essentially, an exaltation of death as life's purposed summit and fulfillment. Here again, there is a shared Hegelian and Nietzschean background. If, as Heidegger argues, history in the traditional, critically evaluated sense is meaningless, then that meaninglessness must be made graphic and shown to be a dead end. In the Hitlerite recomposition of the historical past, in the apocalyptic imperative of a totally new beginning in German destiny, Heidegger could find a confirmation of his own more technical, more esoteric antihistoricism.

But above all, there is the idiom of *Sein und Zeit* and that of the National Socialist jargon. Both, though at obviously different levels, exploit the genius of German for suggestive darkness, its ability to give to (often empty or half-baked) abstractions a physical presence and intensity. There is in Heidegger's supposition, itself at once metaphorical and mesmeric, that it is not man who speaks where language is most fully effective, but "language itself through man," an ominous hint of Hitler's brand of inspiration, of the Nazi use of the human voice as a trumpet played upon by immense, numinous agencies beyond the puny will or judgment of rational man. This motif of dehumanization is key. Nazism comes upon Heidegger precisely at that moment in his thinking when the human person is being edged away from the center of meaning and of being. The idiom of the purely ontological blends with that of the inhuman.

But nauseating as they are, Heidegger's gestures and pronouncements during 1933–34 are tractable. It is his complete silence on Hitlerism and the holocaust after 1945 which is very nearly intolerable.

Every mid-twentieth-century body of serious thought, whether libertarian or conservative, secular or theological, social or psychological, has sought to come to grips with the phenomena of genocide and the concentration camp, with the brusque irruption into the calendar of man of the seasons in hell. The postulate that Auschwitz and Belsen signify some zero-point in the condition and definition of man is now a platitude. For a philosopher, for a German witness, for a thinking, feeling human being implicated in at least a part of the relevant events, to say absolutely nothing is tantamount to complicity. For we are always accomplice to that which leaves us indifferent. Is there, then, anything one can argue to account for or to justify the total silence of one whose later works, according to Martin Buber, "must belong to the ages"?

Only conjecture is possible. Allegations of anti-Semitism are, in respect of the magnitude of the case, trivial, but also, I believe, false. I have been unable to locate anti-Jewish sentiments or utterances in the works of Heidegger, even in those of a public and political nature—a fact, which from the outset, isolates him from the mainstream of Nazism. If Heidegger was, on certain obvious levels, a great man, a teacher whose philosophic-linguistic activity literally towers over various aspects of contemporary speculation, he was, at the same time, a very small man. He led his existence amid a worshipful coterie and, particularly in his later years, behind barriers of adulation. His sorties into the world at large were few and carefully orchestrated. It may well be that he did not have the courage or magnanimity needed to confront his own political past, and the question of Germany's espousal of barbarism. Though engaged in overthrowing traditional metaphysics, though committed to a radical and antiacademic concept of thought, Heidegger was simultaneously a German *Ordinarius*, the lifelong incumbent of a prestigious chair, incapable, either emotionally or intellectually, of facing, of "thinking through," as he would put it, the easy collapse of German academic and cultural institutions before the Nazi challenge.

Moreover, as one ponders Heidegger's career, with its marvelous economy of motion and capacity to generate legend (there are, here, definite points of contact with Wittgenstein's career), the trait that emerges overwhelmingly is that of cunning, of "peasant shrewdness." The pursed mouth and small eyes seem to peer at the questioner out of a millennial legacy of adroit reticence. In view of the facts and of his own part in them, Heidegger may have intuited that a refusal to say anything whatever —even where, especially where he would be pontificating on world politics and American-Soviet materialism—would be, by far, the most effective stance. To which one ought, in fairness, to add the possibility that the enormity of the disaster and of its implications for the continuance of the Western spirit may have seemed to Heidegger, as it has to other writers and thinkers, absolutely beyond rational comment. But he could, at the very least, have said *this*, and the interest he took in the poetry of Celan shows that he was fully aware of the option.

One further hypothesis seems worth testing. Heidegger's involvement with Germany and the German language, in what he takes to be their unique affinity with the dawn of man's being and speech in archaic Greece, is all-determining. It governs his life and work. Germany's pre-eminence in just those activities which may be the highest in reach of man, namely philosophy and music, is a constant theme in German thought and self-awareness. From Bach to Webern, from Kant to Heidegger and Wittgenstein, it is in the German sphere that the genius of man would seem to touch the summits and to plumb the last depths. Given this *Geschick*, this "destined singularity," it could be conceivable that it is from inside the German world also that must spring ultimate inhumanity, the final experiments of man with his own potentiality for destruction. There would be a sense, albeit resistant, indeed offensive, to analytic or pragmatic explanation, in which the possibility of a Bach and of a Beethoven, of a Kant and of a Goethe, would entail—as surely as that of a Wagner and of a Nietzsche—the chance of catastrophe. Embodying "man and superman" or the phenomenon of human identity in its complete spectrum of dialectical extremities, Germany and German history would have the "mittence" of self-destruction, of negation (abstractions for which Hegel and Heidegger had found terms of drastic expression). To offer a critique of this vocation "from beneath," to attempt to circumscribe it within bounds of common sense and morality, would be useless. It would be a trivialization of tragic but exemplary *Dasein*.

Perhaps it was along some such lines (and they are not wholly without force of evidence) that Heidegger thought when he chose to remain mute. Perhaps cunning is a part of fundamental ontology. I do not know. What remains is the cold silence and the abject evasions of Heidegger's followers (among whom Jews are implausibly prominent). What remains, as well, is the question of how this silence, on which Celan seems to touch in his enigmatic poem "Todtnauberg," is to be accorded with the lyric humanity of Heidegger's later writings.

The Presence of Heidegger

III

The *Letter on "Humanism"* sets out the idiom and
motifs that were to dominate Heidegger's postwar
teaching and publications. It is composed in the
evident shadow of national and professional debacle, and is meant to refute Sartre's existentialism, which, albeit derivative from *Sein und Zeit*
at cardinal points, had proclaimed itself to be a
politically engaged "humanism." Heidegger now
postulates the absolute primacy of language:
"Language is the house of Being. Man dwells in
this house. Those who think [*die Denkenden*] and
those who create poetry [*die Dichtenden*] are the
custodians of the dwelling." In *Being and Time*,
the custodianship over being and truth, over authentic existence, was *enacted.* It hinged on the
deed that springs from the supreme liberation of
resolve, of commitment. Now it is not action in any
ordinary sense but thought and poetry that guard,

that alone can realize the presentness and integrity of *Sein*. They, as it were, are the instrumentality and medium of the ontological "letting-be." Thought lets Being be: *das Denken lässt das Sein sein*. Heidegger deliberately borrows the vocabulary of French existentialism in order to underline the difference between his own position and that of his would-be followers. *Denken ist "l'engagement par l'Etre pour l'Etre"* ("thinking is 'the commitment of Being by and for Being' "). The whole relationship of man to speech, of *Dasein* to *Sprache*, is enunciated in a way which does not break with the design of *Sein und Zeit* but which, unquestionably, gives it a new antihumanistic or, more exactly, antianthropocentric twist.

> Language is proper to man, not simply because with his other faculties man also "has" [writes Richardson] the power of speech, but because he has a privileged access to Being. By the same token, the function of his language is simply to let Being be itself. Conversely, it is because other beings do not have this special access to Being that they cannot talk. If the use of language for modern man has become banal, the reason is not to seek on moral or aesthetic grounds but in the fact that the genuine nature of man and his essential relationship to Being remain in oblivion.

But this uniqueness of access is *not* centrality in any Cartesian, Kantian, or Sartrean sense. It is not man who determines Being, but Being that via language discloses itself to and in man. "Thrown into the truth of Being by Being," man is now watchman over this truth. He is the sentinel in the "clearing" or, in one of Heidegger's most celebrated formulations, *der Hirt des Seins* ("the shepherd of Being"). His trusteeship is, ontologically and concretely, the only authentic at-homeness in life, the only genuine indwelling worth striving for in human existence. Hence the Orphic definition: "Language is the irradiant-conceal-ing coming to presentness of Being itself" (*Sprache ist lichtend-verbergende Ankunft des Seins selbst,* in which *lichtend* points to *Lichtung,* "the clearing," and, as we saw, *verbergend* enfolds both "to hide" as in *verbergen,* and "to guard, to lodge securely" as in *bergen*). Man's "thrownness into the clearing of Being," the imposition upon him of the function of watchman and shepherd, renders equally fatuous the Cartesian centrality of the *ego* and the Sartrean scenario of individual existence as the source of freely chosen essence. Man only *is* to the extent that he stands open to Being in what Wordsworth would have called a "wise passiveness."

Heidegger is aware of the strangeness of his own phraseology and argument, of the degree to which his discourse is distancing itself not only from traditional metaphysics and existentialist-humanistic rhetoric but even from the largely diagnostic method of *Sein und Zeit.* Patient in the forest-clearing of Being (now almost invariably hypostatized through its capital letter), dwelling in a house of which he is, at his rare best, a custodian, but never architect or proprietor, the thinker must be prepared to speak seldom, to speak fragmentarily when he speaks at all, and to suffer constant misunderstanding and contradiction. The *Letter on "Humanism"* breaks explicitly with the logic of argument which has structured Western philosophical and scientific thought from Aristotle to modern positivism. Heidegger challenges the very term. If "logic" derives from *logos,* it derives, even more radically, from *legein.* The latter, claims Heidegger, does not signify a discursive, sequential saying, but an in-gathering, a harvesting, a collecting and recollecting (remembering) of the dispersed vestiges of Being. To think fundamentally is not to analyze but to "memorate" (*Denken ist andenken*), to remember Being so as to bring it into radiant disclosure. Such memoration—again Heidegger is strangely close to Plato—is pre-logical. Thus the first law of thought is the "law of Being," not some rule of logic which, in any event, is a late product of the opportunistic-mechanistic impulse, incarnate in Aristotle, to classify beings, to index the world according to man's purposes and convenience. The German language provides Heidegger with an incisive turn: true thinking is *Nachdenken,* the common term for "thinking about," but one in which *Nach-* also means "after," "following upon." The man who "thinks after" is a follower of, an attendant upon the object of his thought, which is Being. His essential stance is one of expectation. It is that "bending toward" of spirit and intellect and ear so uncannily rendered in Fra Angelico's *Annunciation* in San Marco. Richardson, theologically attuned, paraphrases admirably: "Thought, if it is to be true to itself, must be bound only by Being in continual advent toward thought. It must persevere in docility to this continual arrival. It is thus that thought responds to Being's appeal, yields to Being's demands upon it." But although there is quietism and even a strain of Orientalism in this posture (to be developed in a famous dialogue between Heidegger and a Japanese interlocutor, later published in *Poetry, Language, Thought*), there is also a certain readiness for action. Thought is streaming toward us from the disclosing-hiddenness of Being. And it is because "thought is ad-ventive"—Richardson's felicitous transfer—"that it is an enduring adventure."

The *Letter on "Humanism"* concludes by characterizing such adventurous, fundamentally undergone thought as the ideal and object of a future program, of a revolution in *Dasein* infinitely more difficult and penetrating than that called for by existentialist summons to commitment or political insurrection. Later texts, notably *Bauen Wohnen Denken (Building Dwelling Thinking)* of 1951, and the lecture on "Was Heisst Denken" ("What Thinking Signifies") of 1951–52, seek to exemplify and detail the Heideggerian program for a revolution in thought. *Wohnen*, "to dwell in," "to in-habit," is "the fundamental being-structure of *Dasein*." Heidegger derives the verb from Old Saxon *wuon* and Gothic *wunian*, in which he finds the meaning "to tend." Likewise, he finds in *bauen* ("to build") not the notion of novel construction but that of *conservation* (German *hegen*). In German, the farmer *baut* ("builds," "works") his acre; but this acre has been given to him and he is, in plain fact, its custodian and conserver. For once, English can precisely mime the Heideggerian word play. To think is "to attend on Being" but such attendance is a "tending," a "looking after." When thought is present in the inmost of man, it involves far more than "mind" or "brain" —concepts inevitably narrowed by the prestige of logic and scientific method. It implicates what the great mystic Meister Eckhardt called *das Seelenfünklein*, "the little spark or live ember of the soul," and which Heidegger will call "heart." Once more, we are called upon to follow where etymology leads (language knows better than we do). *Cor*, *cordis*, signifying "heart," is central to that process or act of "re-cording" which inspires, which sets alight genuine thinking. Yet a further play on words is decisive, and it too stems from the mystical and Pietist idiom. *Das denken dankt*: "thinking thanks." At its most penetrating, the exercise of thought is one of grateful acquiescence in Being. Inevitably, jubilantly, such acquiescence is a giving of thanks for that which has been placed in our custody, for the light in the clearing. But even more than the thinker, it is the great artist and the poet who are the true celebrants.

Music is almost wholly absent from Heidegger's considerations. I have suggested that this is a drawback, for it is music which might best have instanced two of Heidegger's foremost propositions: the fact that meaning can be plain and compelling but untranslatable into any other code; the extreme difficulty we may encounter in seeking to locate the source of expressive existence, the kernel of existential energy and intelligible occurrence, in a phenomenon or structure that unmistakably *is* right there in front of us. But if music is missing, the visual arts have a distinctive function in Heideggerian ontology.

Der Ursprung des Kunstwerkes (*The Source, the Origin, of the Work of Art*) was written in 1935. It marks a modulation from the technical, even systematic engagement with traditional metaphysics in *Sein und Zeit* to the "poetics" of Heidegger's later approach. The question of the nature of truth, of the dynamics of hiddenness and unconcealment through which *Dasein* experiences or, more exactly, "suffers," "undergoes" truth, had been posed repeatedly in *Sein und Zeit*. But the counters of discussion had been more or less those of customary philosophy, and the question itself had remained unresolved. In this irresolution, Heidegger had come to perceive the larger dilemma of the inability of ordered verbal discourse to overcome metaphysical constraints and pierce to the core of things. Now it is just this piercing which seems to characterize great, authentic art. Indeed, truth itself, *das Wesen der Wahrheit in sich selbst,* the dynamics of radiant in-dwelling, "come into being" and "achieve realization and self-possession" (*ereignen sich*) in the work of art. How can this be? What is the source of this eventuation?

"The artist is the source of the work. The work is the source of the artist. Neither is without the other." Both are the product of "the truth of Being," as it were; they are the active, generative locus in and through which this truth is manifest. Heidegger writes: "In the work of art, the truth of Being is at work," and the German idiom *ins Werk gesetzt* allows him the twofold sense of "being at work" and "being inside a work." We experience this operative presence in a context that is beginning to differ significantly from the pragmatic solidity of *Sein und Zeit*. The latter bore on facticity and immediate matter. The immediacy of and to matter was that of human use: wood signified lumber, the mountain entailed the quarry. It was, furthermore, a world in which presentness was being continually absorbed by and into the more ontologically privileged temporalities of *Gewesenheit* ("pastness") and *gewesende Zukunft* ("future in being"). But a more searching reflection on ontological *Angst* and on "nothingness" has shown us that the world exists in a more absolute and nonpragmatic sense. It has shown us that the presentness in things has its own integral, "ecstatic" authority. To identify this nonpragmatic, nonutilitarian presence and ecstasy, Heidegger coins the verb *zu welten*. In and through the work of art, with its disinterestedly creative yet dependent relationship to wood, stone, or pigment, with its total presentness in yet also out of historical time, the world *weltet* (untranslatably, "the world worlds"). And it is just this mode of existentiality which turns out to be fundamental.

Heidegger meditates on (*denkt-nach*) van Gogh's painting of an old, worn-out pair of shoes. It is not some antecedent, Platonic knowledge that we have of the nature of such an object that enables us to grasp, to undergo the realization of, van Gogh's presentment. On the contrary: it is van Gogh's canvas that makes it possible for us to experience the integral reality, the innermost quiddity and meaning of the two shoes. Scientific analysis would proceed via decomposition; however exhaustive its findings on the relevant chemistry of leather or on the history of shoes in general or in particular, the result would be a dead abstraction. The knowledge which comes of *praxis*, the knowledge possessed by the wearer of these shoes, is, as *Sein und Zeit* underlined, invaluable. But it is *interested* knowledge, it *uses* the object of its insight. *Only art lets-be.* Only in and through the painting does the pair of shoes achieve a total, autonomous being *per se*. Long after the object is of no more scientific interest or of no more practical use ("these shoes are fit only to be thrown away"), the existential inscape and living presence of the pair is preserved and guarded in the painting. Far beyond any pair of shoes we encounter in "real life," it is van Gogh's work that communicates to us the essential "shoeness," the "truth of being" of these two leather shapes— shapes at once infinitely familiar and, when we step back from facticity and "open ourselves to Being," infinitely new and uncanny.

It is art that allows the later Heidegger to delineate, to make as palpable as he can, the antinomy of truth's simultaneous hiddenness and self-deployment. It is art that enacts the dialectical reciprocity of cloture and radiance. The essence of "thereness" and of meaning that a great painting or sculpture reveals, exhibits, makes sensible is, obviously, "within-it." It is embodied in the substance of the thing. We cannot externalize it or extract it from the work's specific mass and configuration. In this sense, it is a hiddenness. But such embodiment is, at the very same instant, a making manifest, a deployment, an articulate and radiant projection. *"In der Un-verborgenheit waltet die Verbergung"* ("In unconcealment dwells hiddenness and safekeeping"). In the Heideggerian aesthetic, creation and safekeeping, composition and conservation are absolutely indivisible. Even the most revolutionary work of art, if it is authentic, will conserve and give to Being a dwelling and a sanctuary such as it can find nowhere else.

Here Heidegger's example is that of a Greek temple. The temple is earth-rooted and has, literally, sprung from the earth. Now it conceals the earth beneath it while, simultaneously, linking it to the sky. Inside the temple the deity is at once present and absent, made manifest in epiphany yet hidden from view. The temple, as a colonnaded space, is both open to the outside and enclosed. In a Greek temple the two primordial agencies of the truth of Being—openness, die *Lichtung*, and concealment or guarded infolding—conjoin. The sky is, in this new Heideggerian parlance, the place and realization of openness. The earth is the locale of concealment and sanctified in-habitation (*der Verbergung als Bergung*). Both are indispensable if existence is to find authentic embodiment (the Shakespearean "bodying forth" is what Heidegger aims at).

But such simultaneity and conjunction are polemical. Here Heidegger invokes the notion of vital strife (*polemos*) derived from Heraclitus. In the great work of art, hiddenness and exhibition—the absence of the object itself and its intense presence via the artist's representation—are in eternal conflict. The work of art shows us that "truth happens in the guise of the primordial struggle between 'clearance' and concealment." And once again, the heart of Heidegger's meaning—with its brilliant refutation of the Platonic derogation of artistic *mimesis* as a mendacious, secondhand form—lodges in a play on words. Art is a *Stiftung*, which term signifies an instauration or foundation (as of a temple), a bestowal upon. This instauration comes of the artist's *Schöpfung*, or "creation." But if *schöpfen* means "to create," it means also, and for Heidegger more authentically, "to draw from a well." Thus the artist's work is a literal "drawing up to the light from the well of being," which well is sunk in the guardian earth.

The charged nothingness from which Being springs ("the wellspring") lodges in the hidden deeps. To create is to bring to light, but in a way which is a consecration (a *Stiftung*), because what is brought to light is also to be guarded—as man guards or ought to guard the earth from which he draws sustenance and on which he builds. The fount and meaning of true art is *"die schaffende Bewahrung der Wahrheit"* ("the creative custodianship of the truth"). Art is not, as in Plato or Cartesian realism, an imitation of the real. It is the more real. And Heidegger's penetration of this paradox leaves traditional aesthetics far behind.

Creation *should be* custody; a human construction *should be* the elicitation and housing of the great springs of being. But we know that reality is otherwise. Technology has ravaged the earth and degraded natural forms to mere utility. Man has labored and thought not with but against the grain of things. He has not given lodging to the forces and creatures of the natural world but made them homeless. Today, penitential ecology and attempts at reparation, probably futile, are a mounting element in social sensibility and the politics of disgust. But Heidegger came much earlier. His advocacy of the sanctity of the environment and of what ought to be our trusteeship of earth and organisms, moreover, is grounded neither in pseudotheology nor in political radicalism (with its provenance from Rousseau). When Heidegger cites the rootedness of existence in the actual contours of the ground, when he summons to remembrance the autonomous life of organic and inorganic matter, its aura and irreducible immanence, when he identifies authentic creation and edification with the bringing to light of precedent energies and truths—he is on rigorously philosophic ground. His model of the numinous fourfold interplay between the "gods," mankind, the heavens, and the earth is a development, metaphoric no doubt, but consequent nonetheless, of the analysis of *Dasein* and the program of

fundamental ontology. This development necessarily involves a critique of the entire concept of technology.
Though made public only in 1953, *Die Frage Nach der
Technik* (*"The Question [Questioning] of Technology"*)
embodies arguments and reflections which go back to
Sein und Zeit. What is novel and inhibiting is the dense
idiosyncrasy of Heidegger's later idiom.

Once, says Heidegger, nature was *phusis,* the archaic
designation of natural reality which he reads as contain-
ing within itself the Greek sense for "coming into radiant
being" (as it is still faintly discernible in our word "phenomenon"). *Phusis* proclaimed the same process of creation that generates a work of art. It was, in the best sense,
poiesis—a making, a bringing forth. The blossom breaking from the bud and unfolding into its proper being
(*en eautō*) is, at once, the realization of *phusis* and of
poiesis, of organic drive—Dylan Thomas's "green fuse"—
and of the formal creative-conservative dynamism which
we experience in art. Originally, *technē* had its pivotal
place in this complex of meanings and perceptions. It
also sprang from an understanding of the primacy of
natural forms and from the cardinal Greek insight that
all "shaping," all construction of artifacts, is a focused
knowing. A "technique" is a mode of knowledge which
generates this or that object, it is a re-cognition toward
truthful ends. (Something of the Heideggerian reticulation can be made out in the cognate range, in English,
of "craft" and of "cunning," with their respective derivation from Germanic roots for "knowing" and "forming.")
No less than art, *technē* signified a bringing into true
being, a making palpable and luminous, of that which is
already inherent in *phusis.* Heidegger's word for authentic
technology is *entbergen.* German supports an incisive
double and even contradictory reading: *zu entbergen* can

mean either "to reveal" or "to guard in hiddenness." As we have seen, both motions are essential in man's commerce with the truth of being.

But with the fatal revolution of values that Heidegger ascribes to the Platonic demeaning of natural objects and human products and to the Aristotelian-Cartesian mastery over knowledge or, more precisely, use of knowledge in order to exercise mastery, the original meaning of *techne* has been debased. Heidegger's examples are characteristic. Where rural existence is still in concord with the world the farmer's "technique" is not a *provocation* of the earth. It is a donation (sowing), an acceptance (harvest), a perennial custodianship and instauration. The dam across the living stream, on the contrary, is an enslavement and deconstruction. The energies and natural lineaments of the river are coerced through artificial apertures into the servitude of turbines. Flora and fauna go to ruin in the inert reservoir behind the dam. Heidegger qualifies this proceeding as *das Ungeheure*. The term is of drastic force. It signifies the "uncannily monstrous." It is *provocation* (*das Herausfordern*) which distinguishes the original life-giving and life-enhancing meaning of "technique" (the Lawrentian vocabulary is, here, almost inevitable) from the modern sense and uses of technology. These, says Heidegger, are mounting to a mad climax in the United States and the Soviet Union—societies of which he had, as it happens, no direct knowledge. The "planetary technology" which these two superpowers harness and disseminate (the phrase stems from the conservative nationalist writer and thinker Ernst Jünger) far transcends apparent ideological differences. Capitalism and state-communism are merely variants in a common technicity and exploitation of nature. It is, hints Heidegger, Europe's final mittence to preserve what vestiges there are of authentic *techne*. In this preservation Europe's relative weakness and tragic history could be instrumental.

True art, true knowledge, true technique are a "vocation," a "calling forth" that imposes upon man his native "calling." Since Roman engineering and seventeenth-century rationalism, Western technology has not been a vocation but a provocation and imperialism. Man challenges nature, he harnesses it, he compels his will on wind and water, on mountain and woodland. The results have been fantastic. Heidegger knows this: he is no Luddite innocent or pastoralist dropout. What he is emphasizing is the price paid. *Things*, with their intimate, collaborative affinity with creation, have been demeaned into *objects*. The German word is *Gegenstände*, which, literally and marvelously to Heidegger's purpose, signifies that which "stands against," which "affronts." We may, on the levels of utility and abstraction, have made ourselves lords of creation. But the elements of the natural world have become *Gegenstände*. They stand against us. Our relationship to and with them is, to use a sociological tag, "an adversary relationship," a confrontation. We are alienated from that which we decompose and exploit, as the Hegelian master is alienated from his indispensable servant. Of the two vital senses of *Entbergung* we have retained only the coercive, the literally extractive. We have compelled nature to yield knowledge and energy, but we have given to nature, to that which is live and hidden within it, no patient hearing, no in-dwelling. Thus our technologies mask Being instead of bringing it to light.

To represent this masking, Heidegger uses the term *Gestell*. In it he concentrates the sterile, mendacious connotations of "scaffold," "gimmick," and "armature." Trapped in the technological *Gestell*, Being is not made radiant, it is not housed but, on the contrary, *verwahrlost* ("wasted," "made tawdry," "falsified"). And whatever the miracles of engineering, moon-landings included, the consequences for man are destructive. It is around *Gestell* that Heidegger weaves his punitive net. Man orders nature to do his rapacious bidding ("to order" is *zu bestellen*). But nature and the *Gegenstände* riposte in an inevitable dialectic. They conceal their authentic being and make man false to the world ("to be false to," "to assume a lying stance" is *sich zu verstellen*). Thus *Bestellengestellen-verstellen*—"to command–construct artificially–deceive and self-deceive"—form one of those Heideggerian assonant-consonant clusters in which a whole vision and critique are made articulate.

Our dissociation of the negative from the positive values of *technē* and our violent deflection of "vocation" into "provocation" have made us homeless on the earth. Technology is now, in many aspects, a nightmare that threatens to enslave or even destroy its begetter. The debate over the atom bomb, says Heidegger almost contemptuously, is a journalistic footnote to a crisis whose real source is "the forgetting of Being" at the ambiguous inception of Western intellectual history. It is a late, vulgar episode in a process of alienation between man and world that goes back to the substitution of *Einblick* for Heraclitean *Einblitz*—an untranslatable play on words that Heidegger makes in 1959 to differentiate rationalistic-scientific "insight" from the lightning bolt of true penetration.

Yet to understand this tragic process, and to realize that false technicity has edged the human race to the brink of ecological devastation and political suicide, is to realize also that salvation is possible, that it *must* be possible. It is precisely because exploitative technology and the worship of allegedly objective science are the natural culmination of Western metaphysics after Plato, that the Heideggerian summons "to overcome metaphysics" is, simultaneously and quintessentially, a summons "to the saving of the earth." The two are indissoluble. It is in the very extremis of the modern crisis, the very time of nihilistic mechanism, that hope lies ready. Heidegger's essay concludes with a quotation from Hölderlin:

> *Wo aber Gefahr ist, wächst*
> *Das Rettende auch.*

("But where there is danger, there also grows the strength, the agency of salvation.")

The fatality of technicity lies in the fact that we have broken the links between *technē* and *poiesis*. It is time we turned to the poets.

We have seen that literary influences were not absent from Heidegger's early work. But it is only in the mid-1930s, under stress of public events and in the conviction that the language of *Sein und Zeit* had proved inadequate to its innovative, revolutionary purpose, that Heidegger turned fully to Hölderlin. The four readings of Hölderlin that Heidegger gave in the guise of lectures and essays between 1936 and 1944 make up one of the most disconcerting, spellbinding documents in the history of Western literary and linguistic sensibility. Spoken against a backdrop of deepening barbarism and national self-destruction, these commentaries on a number of Hölderlin's major hymns are nothing less than an endeavor to pierce, via a singular kind of textual and critical exegesis, to the last sanctuary of poetic invention, national identity, and human speech itself. As in the resplendent second chorus of Sophocles' *Antigone*, of which he has published an often arbitrary but profoundly suggestive interpretation, so Heidegger finds in Hölderlin one of those very rare, immeasurably important expressions of man's fallenness, of his ostracism from Being and the

gods, and, simultaneously, a statement of this very condition whose truth and lyric power give assurance of rebirth.

It is in Hölderlin's "Heimkunft" and "Wie wenn am
Feiertag . . ." that the hidden, occluded truth of Being
literally re-enters into the house of man. The theme of
pilgrimage and festive procession in the two hymns enacts a fundamental ontological homecoming. Because he
is the "active occasion," the incarnate "clearing" in which
Sein deploys its radiant enclosedness, the supreme poet—
Pindar, Sophocles, Hölderlin—is pre-eminently the shepherd of Being. In the midst of a nihilism and waste of
spirit of which his own vulnerable social and psychological
status make him the most acute and also the most endangered of witnesses, it is the poet who, supremely,
perhaps even alone, is guarantor of man's ultimate *Heim-
kehr* ("homecoming") to natural truth, to a sanctified
hearth in the world of beings. (In the closing lines of the
Antigone-chorus Heidegger "hears" the implicit, never-
to-be exhausted evocation of this hearth.) It is the poet's
calling—literal, soul-consuming, imperative to the point
of personal ruin—to bring creation into the neighborhood
of the divine. For though the gods have left the earth—
Hölderlin hymns their going—and though they have
abandoned it to its spoilers, they are near still, and light
upon it in ardent visitation. Of these, it is the poet who
is the immediate object. It is he whom lightning seeks.
He must receive the hammering fire and give it lodging.
But he can do so only briefly and at ultimate risk. Hence
Hölderlin's inspired unreason, hence the existential disaster that so often attends on great creative genius—be
it Hölderlin's or van Gogh's. It is, furthermore, Hölderlin's own gloss on Antigone as a being doomed by the
proximity of the gods into which she has been thrust by
her hunger for absolute truth and pure justice that in-

spires Heidegger's image of the poet as one similarly doomed by his intimacy with the divine.

But although he may part with his reason and his very life, the poet has held *Sein* in his pastoral guard, and this capture or, rather, reception and offertory acceptance, illumines, validates, and underwrites man's potential in a way that no theology, no metaphysics, no scientific theory, no technological wonder can equal. Authentic poetry, which is exceedingly rare, is "the real estate, the fundamental resource on earth, of man's habitation" (*"das Grundvermögen des menschlichen Wohnens"*). It is Hölderlin, the driven wanderer, the pilgrim into madness who, of all men, was most at home.

Hölderlin scholars, notably Bernhard Böschenstein, have no difficulty in showing that Heidegger's readings are very often indefensible. By etymologizing individual words and phrases, as he does in his own philosophical arguments, by using unreliable or fragmented texts, Heidegger imposes on Hölderlin a strain of nationalist mystique for which the actual poems give little support, and which is the uglier in view of the dates at which Heidegger put forward his gloss. Moreover, Heidegger arbitrarily extends to Hölderlin's earlier works ambiguities of intention and lexical-syntactical idiosyncrasies that only appear in the poet's late, partially "benighted" utterances. Here, as in his notorious "translations" from the pre-Socratics, Heidegger is carrying to violent extremes the hermeneutic paradox whereby the interpreter "knows better" than his author, whereby interpretation, where it is inspired and probing enough, can "go behind" the visible text to the hidden roots of its inception and meaning. This, undoubtedly, is how Heidegger operates, and on the level of normal expository responsibility many of his readings are opportunistic fictions.

But not always. Heidegger's commentary on Stefan

George's poem "Das Wort" (in a lecture so entitled and delivered in 1958) seems to me incomparable in its penetration and finesse. If he augments the fitful, reiterative texture of the poems of Georg Trakl, Heidegger's reading of "Ein Winterabend" (in the essay *Die Sprache* of 1950) is, nevertheless, a marvel of sympathy. Heidegger's analysis of Trakl's oblique uses of tense and of epithets as predicate will stand. The parallel reading of the *Antigone*-chorus, of which Hölderlin had made a famous "metamorphic" rendering, is of a seriousness and appropriateness to its object of which there are few rival examples in the history of classical scholarship and criticism. Heidegger's proceeding here is analogous to that of Dante when the narrator places, and thus gives new illumination to, a Virgilian or Provençal precedent.

Heidegger is not aiming at textual fidelity in the customary sense. He is attempting to seize, to make audible the presence of Being in that uncanny hazard of total rightness, of time-rooted intemporality which we experience as, which we know to be (but *how* do we know?) a great poem. He is striving to articulate the paradox, evident in Trakl's best work, through which exceedingly simple, naked words enter into, generate a construct, a music of thought, of insight into the meaning of life which are, literally and demonstrably, *inexhaustible*. These enigmas of intrinsic gravity, of "everlastingness," of a sum of significance immensely in excess of its manifest constituent parts, are at the heart of poetry and of man's invention of and response to literature. The bulk of textual interpretation and literary criticism leaves them intact or relegates them to a category of reverent cliché. Heidegger faces them head-on. Hence the strangeness and strained "irresponsibility" of some of his findings.

Behind the particular exegesis lies the imperative vision. The poet's speech *stiftet das Bleibende* ("grounds," "initiates," or "guards," "the enduring"). The poet re-enacts the primordial *Schöpfung* performed by the gods. Such re-enactment entails proximity and rivalry. In some perilous sense the poet is a re-creator who challenges the absent gods, who does their work for them, albeit under the lightning bolt of their spendthrift and jealous visitations. The nerve of poetry is the act of *nomination*. Authentic poetry does not "imitate," as Plato would have it, or "represent" or "symbolize," as post-Aristotelian literary theory supposes. *It names*, and by naming makes it real and lasting. The underlying motif here, familiar to Pietist thought, is of Adam's nomination in the Garden of every living thing. When Hölderlin names the Rhine, he neither imitates nor represents it: he "speaks it" in a nomination which gives to it precisely that unfolding, lasting verity and presentness which the builder of dams and the hydrographer decompose and destroy. There can be no valid difference, says Heidegger, between "the poem" and "that which is the poem" (i.e., between the river and Hölderlin's hymn).

Via Sophocles' "openness to the summons of Being," the Sophoclean Antigone herself becomes, herself is "the homecoming, the becoming housed in the condition of unhousedness." And this homecoming, which only the naming by the poet can perform and predicate, enables man to glimpse—to undergo by means of metaphoric prevision, as it were—his own entrance into the dwelling of death. "Mankind dwells poetically, in the condition of poetry" (*"Dichterisch wohnet der Mensch"*), wrote Hölderlin in a late poem. Heidegger expounds this saying in a lecture in 1952. He sees in it the ultimate, probably the only, hope for a way out from the nihilism of the age. The poet names what is holy; or, rather, his nomination calls from hiddenness, without doing violence to it, that which is still alive in the grimed earth. Poetry is not language in some esoteric, decorative, or occasional guise. It is the essence of language where language *is*, where man is *bespoken*, in the antique, strong sense of the word.

Heidegger's meditations on language and logic go back to a paper of 1912 ("*Neue Forschungen über Logik*"). His encounter with Hölderlin, Sophocles, Rilke, brings the poetic essence of all true speech into the center of his thought. Obsessed with instrumentality, with informational functionality, language has lost the genius of nomination and in-gathering as it is explicit in the original meaning of *logos*. *Denken* and *dichten*, "to think" and "to create poetry," are the two avenues of the *logos*. "The thinker says Being. The poet names what is holy." In "Das Ereignis" ("The Event"), an unpublished paper of 1941, Heidegger anchors both *dichten* and *denken* in *danken*. To think, to write a poem, is to give thanks for whatever measure of homecoming to Being is open to mortal man. But whereas Heidegger is not certain whether the language of even the best thought can escape from its rationalistic-deterministic imprint—a doubt which he explores sharply in *Identität und Differenz* (*Identity and Difference*) of 1957—he *is* confident that *Sein* has found its dwelling and its celebration in the work of the great poets.

It does seem to me that Heidegger is, at certain moments, a reader of poetry like no other in our time, a re-enactor of the poem's genesis and meaning who towers above the tired bric-a-brac of literary criticism and academic commentary. Linguistics and the understanding of literature have until now scarcely begun to grasp the wealth and consequence of his proposals.

At the outset, I emphasized that the scope of this book precludes any attempt at an adequate assessment of Heidegger's status. So does the bare fact that a large portion of his writings is, as yet, unpublished. A tentative estimate ought, nonetheless, to be put forward.

The first point to be urged is this: despite the deliberate singularity of its style, which one will experience as repellent or fascinating or as an unsettling mixture of both, and despite the lived and legend-wrought apartness of Heidegger's biography, the fundamental ontology which Heidegger proposes is not some erratic bloc in an otherwise unrelated setting. It is at many and decisive points a part of a larger, fully recognizable movement of feeling.

Heidegger's diagnosis of individual alienation in modern society and of the anguish which is both the symptom and corrective of this "fallenness" and dehumanization has an unmistakable twofold provenance. It derives, first, from the great lineage of pessimism and admonition in Augustinian Christianity. Heidegger's reading of man links closely with that of Augustine, Luther, Pascal, and Kierkegaard. In a very real sense, *Sein und Zeit* is a twentieth-century *reprise* and elaboration of Kierkegaard's *Either/Or* and *Fear and Trembling*. The partial break and originality will only come when Heidegger queries the centrality of man and of human consciousness in the truth of *Dasein*. The second main source of Heidegger's critique of the values and tenor of individual existence in a materialistic, mass-consumer society is, of course, sociological. It draws, either implicitly or explicitly, on Durkheim's concept of *anomie*, on sociological analyses of the erosion of personal autonomy through the industrial process and, above all, on Marx. As Reinhart Maurer and Lucien Goldmann have shown, Heidegger's awareness of Marxism is extensive even where, or precisely where, it is most contrastive and even polemic. It is difficult to imagine some of Heidegger's most representative pages on the depersonalization of twentieth-century urban man or on the exploitative, basically imperialist motivation in Western science and technology, without the immediate precedent of *Das Kapital* and of Engels' indictments of industrial inhumanity.

In turn, Heidegger's work, even where it is branded as obscurantist or worse, will strongly influence the entire neo-Marxist critique of consumer-ethics, of man's enslavement by technology, and of the ingestion of the individual in the "lonely crowd." Marcuse's "one-dimensional man" is a variant on Heidegger's more far-reaching notion of "theyness." Lukács's key idea of the decadence from classic realism—an authentic experiencing of the truth and of the world—to the helpless acceptance of mechanistic determinism in "naturalism," is closely parallel with Heidegger's distinction between authentic and inauthentic mundanity. The neo-Marxist ideal of a new "humanized technology," of a return to harmonic concordance between human needs and the laws of production, is pure Heidegger. He too calls for a "technology of responsibility," for a reversion to the classical scale of the human person. Even where Heidegger is most dismissive of Marxism, and where he advocates a "far more radical conception of overthrow" (namely, the overthrow of Western metaphysics and the return to a remembrance of Being), he is closely in tune with the revisionist, partly messianic Marxism of the 1920s. The echoes are substantial between *Sein und Zeit* and the writings both of Ernst Bloch and of the "meta-Marxists" of the Frankfurt School. The young Lukács too draws on Kierkegaard. A shared climate of anguish and utopia is instrumental.

But Heidegger's espousal of a "new technology" remains unconvincing. He is an agrarian through and through. Field and forest are at the heart of the Heideggerian world. The woodsman and the farmer, acting in immemorial affinity with their surroundings, provide

Heidegger with a touchstone of existential rightness. And here again, Heideggerian language and thought fit readily into a much larger spectrum. Agrarian reaction and pastoral nostalgia play a part in modern ideology. Heidegger's rebuke to rootlessness, his distaste for the metropolitan and the cosmopolitan, can be exactly matched not merely in National Socialist writings but in those of Barrès and Péguy. Heidegger's invocation of the tenebrous strengths that man must draw from the veins of the earth, his scarcely veiled belief in the mystery of blood and ethnic destiny, his contempt for the mercantile, can be exactly paralleled in the vision of D. H. Lawrence and the vocabulary of Jünger or Gottfried Benn. When Heidegger exalts the antique fitness of landed ways, when he responds fervently to the aura of handcrafts and scorns the tawdry veneer of marketplace and *bourse,* he is in perfect accord with a range of intuitions and doctrines that extends from Yeats and the Fugitive movement in the American South all the way to Ortega y Gasset (an early admirer) and F. R. Leavis's wheelwright's shop. All these motions of spirit tell of the same revolt against mercantile liberalism, the same hankering after "antique harvesters." They modulate from Rousseau, and their political ends are those of reaction. Heidegger's addendum to this large school of anger and reverie is the belief, partly metaphoric, that the ancient deities, or the agencies of vital order which they image, are inherent in earth and in forest and that they can be resurrected and induced into dynamic play. (The earth, says Heidegger, must once again be made a *Spielraum,* literally, "a space in which to play.")

Heidegger's "primalism," his obsessive plea for a return to a truth of being, of thought, of utterance, which he locates (again, I think, in part metaphorically) in archaic pre-Socratic Greece, is undoubtedly one of the most arresting, personal elements in his ontology. But here as well he does not stand alone. As he himself insists, the attempt to overturn traditional metaphysics and to set aside the errors of Platonic idealism and Aristotelian positivism is grounded in the Nietzschean polemic against Socrates, in the Nietzschean dialectic of the struggle between Apollonian and Dionysian forces. It is Heidegger's contention that Nietzsche did not go far enough, that the "will to power" is not a transcendence of Western metaphysics but, on the contrary, its natural and nihilistic climax. But Heidegger's own thought carries forward from Nietzsche's. And when Heidegger intimates a condition of language in which the word was immediate to the truth of things, in which light shone through words instead of being fogged or bent by their dusty use, he echoes exactly Mallarmé's quip made in 1894 (and, in fact, referred to by Heidegger in one of his late texts) that "all poetry has gone wrong since the great Homeric deviation." Where Heidegger posits a numinous verity of language in Anaximander, Parmenides, and Heraclitus, Mallarmé names Orpheus—of whom, to be sure, no word has survived. The degree to which this "primalism," this axiomatic intuition of an earlier stage of authenticity in human affairs—which Heidegger shares with the Marx of the 1848 manuscripts, with the Freud of *Totem and Taboo*, and with the Lévi-Strauss of *Mythologiques*— represents a secular variant on the scenario of Eden and Adam's fall is an absolutely pivotal question. Its investigation would lead to the root of modern culture.

It is because Heidegger's work, for all its idiosyncrasy, does relate at so many junctures to preceding and contemporary movements, that its impact has, in turn, been so rapid and widespread. It has been felt even by those philosophers whose own aims and methods differ radically from Heidegger's. In two remarkable papers, K. O.

Apel has shown how real are the areas of contact between Wittgenstein's and Heidegger's emphasis on everydayness, how illuminating are the analogies between Heidegger's "ontological difference" and Wittgenstein's separation of that which can be said from that which cannot. Others have remarked on the devaluation of formal logic common to Heidegger's and Wittgenstein's critiques of linguistic positivism, and it has too often been forgotten that Gilbert Ryle's review of *Sein und Zeit* in *Mind* (1929) was thoroughly receptive. Yet others have found in John Dewey's antitraditionalism near affinities to Heidegger. In other words, the extent of Heidegger's penetration into the current of even those philosophies most overtly hostile to his own enterprise may be considerable. It is too early to tell.

Its impact on postwar existentialism, on the other hand, has been overwhelming. Sartre's philosophic writings are, in essence, commentaries on *Sein und Zeit*. The entire repertoire of "engagement," "commitment," "taking upon oneself," "freedom of being," "authenticity," "the inalienability of one's death," in Sartre, Camus, and their innumerable epigones is Heideggerian in root and branch. The influence on theology has been almost comparable. Via Karl Rahner on the Catholic side, via Bultmann on the Protestant, Heidegger's ontology, the concept of the seminal ambiguity of man's "fallenness into the world," the Heideggerian hermeneutic or way of seeking to "hear" the *pneuma*, the breath of hidden spirit in language, have had tremendous influence. Reciprocally, theology has claimed Heidegger for its own.

The Heideggerian analysis of "theyness," the idea that the individual must accomplish his own freedom in relation to death, has been taken up by such psychoanalysts as M. Boss and L. Binswanger. The current schools of "existentialist therapy" in Switzerland and in the United

States are Heideggerian in source and method. So is the psychoanalytic linguistics of Lacan and his French disciples (notably that of Derrida), through whose work Heidegger is exercising profound influence on French literary thought. The Heideggerian poetics of a scholar such as Emil Staiger have been severely attacked by Walter Muschg, but these poetics are beginning to tell throughout the field of German and East European theories of literature. Harder to pin down, but palpable, are the effects which Heidegger's manner and outlook have had on the actual poetry and prose of Ilse Aichinger, of Ingeborg Bachmann, of René Char, and, above all, of Paul Celan, one of the greatest voices in European poetry after Mallarmé and Rilke.

Severely disputed as it is, Heidegger's way of interpreting the pre-Socratics and Sophocles has found convinced followers: among them, Karl Reinhardt and Kurt Riezler in Germany, H. Bollack in France, Donald Carne-Ross in the United States. In a more general compass, the hermeneutics, the model of textual understanding developed in Hans-Georg Gadamer's *Truth and Method*, itself now so widely influential, is developed explicitly out of Heidegger's concept and practice of language. In a striking essay of 1949, C. F. von Weizsäcker even went so far as to assert that Heidegger's teachings on a "science of acceptance," that Heidegger's critique of the Cartesian ideal of abstractive appropriation, have a valid bearing on the more recent, "subjective" aspect of particle physics. The physicist, too, must learn to "listen" and to accept his trusteeship of Being.

Thus there is, just now, hardly a sphere of intellectual argument and language-consciousness in which the presence of Martin Heidegger is not manifest—be it only as a force to be exorcised. The often-voiced supposition that Heidegger will throw his shadow over later twentieth-century thought as did Nietzsche over sensibility at the beginning of the century does not seem baseless.

But this, finally, is not the issue.

Where does one stand on the Heideggerian claim to have thought or, at the least, to have initiated "the thinking of Being"? What, so far as can be said today, is the status of Heidegger's "fundamental ontology"? Heidegger himself knew that this was the question on which the validity of his lifework hinged. He came back to it or, rather, sought to give it final clarification, in four colloquia held between September 1966 and September 1973.

He retraces his steps. *Sein und Zeit* was not meant to arrive at a new definition of Being. It was meant to prepare *Dasein* "to apprehend, to hear the word of Being." Its purpose was to make *Dasein* accessible to the supreme existential question. But even this preparation makes manifest the cardinal fact of ontological difference: Being is not itself an extant, it is not something that can simply be identified with or deduced from particular beings (*"das Sein ist nicht seiend"*). To inquire into Being is not to ask: What is *this* or *that*? It is to ask: What is "is" (*"was ist das 'ist'"*)? Even to ask is to realize that this question has not been posed nakedly in Western thought since the pre-Socratics and that Western systematic philosophy has, indeed, done everything to conceal the question. But it is also to realize that human speech, either through some inherent limitation or because the impress upon it of conventional logic and rational grammar is too incisive, cannot give an answer that simultaneously *answers to,* is authentically *answerable to,* the nature of the question, *and* satisfies normal criteria of intelligibility. This, says Heidegger, leaves only the resort to tautology.

But need we reject this form? Must we equate a tautologous definition with meaningless circularity or emptiness? No, replies Heidegger, at this tranquil, summarizing moment in his lifework. So-called logical, so-called analytical objectivity, the arrogant claims of positivism and the illusions of verifiability/falsifiability (Popper's model) have led Western man to personal alienation and collective barbarism. His proud scientific-technological world is one of underlying despair and absurdity. Thus it may well be that the "tautologous is the sole possibility we have of thinking, of thinking through, that which dialectics can only conceal." We cannot paraphrase *is*. We cannot explicate the *"isness"* of Being. We can only state it tautologically: *Sein ist Sein* ("Being is Being").

And the very late Heidegger goes even further or "darker." Being is neither a substance nor an agency nor an occult force. It is "everything," but it is also, in respect to its source, indivisibly implicit in *nothingness*, in that *Nichts* which, as Carnap and A. J. Ayer scornfully pointed out, can be neither defined nor verified, but which all of us, riposts Heidegger, know at first hand in moments of anguish and vertigo. We can write *Sein: Nichts*, says Heidegger. But this equation is not negative. The *Nichts* is not *nihil*. Nothingness is not negation of Being. The very word teaches us that: *no-thing-ness* signifies a presentness, an existential "thereness" which is not naïvely enclosed in or circumscribed by any particular extant, specific object. *"Das Nichten des Nichts 'ist' das Sein"*: *"the negation of nothingness 'is' Being."* To Carnap such a sentence is the final proof of Heidegger's vacuity. To Heidegger it is an attempt, inevitably tautological, to re-educate language and thought—they are the same— toward the tasks of ontological understanding and man's survival on this earth (these, too, are the same). It is only when it will be able to abide the paradoxicality, the scandalous strangeness and, from any ordinary philosophic-scientific point of view, the ridiculousness of this task that *Dasein* will have found its way home.

Even so scrupulously sympathetic a reader of Heidegger as Winfried Franzen concludes that "any clear determination of what Heidegger actually means by *Sein* is, up to now, virtually impossible." In this perspective, the final recourse to tautology would be an inescapable admission of defeat. And this may, indeed, be the case. At one moment in *Identität und Differenz*—unique, so far as I am aware, in Heidegger's whole writings—the master concedes with brusque humor that the ontological quest, the attempt to separate Being from beings, is a sort of futile game, a circular catch-as-catch-can. Even this, of course, would not necessarily mean that the game had not been worth playing, that it did not engage the most bracing and ennobling of human impulses. But it would be a bleak tally.

There can, however, be another approach to the tautological core of Martin Heidegger's philosophy of Being. *Sein ist Sein* and the rejection of paraphrase or logical exposition have their exact precedent in the ontological finality of theology. Formally, as we have seen, they are the absolute equivalent to the Self-utterance and Self-definition of the Deity—*I am that which I am*—and to the refusal, as complete in Kant as it is in the Old Testament itself, to anatomize, to decompose analytically the transcendent oneness of the divine. Heidegger is determined to think outside theology. He insists that his fundamental ontology is extratheological, that it has absolutely nothing to tell us, either way, of the existence or attributes of God. It is, however, my own experience that Heidegger's paradigm and expression of Being, of the ontological cut between Being and beings, adapts at almost every point to the substitution of "God" for the term

Sein. This *does not* prove that such substitution is latent in Heidegger's design. He would repudiate it. But it does mean, to this reader at least, that the philosophy, the sociology, the poetics and, at some opaque level, the politics of Heidegger embody and articulate an "after-" or "post-theology."

Such "post-theologies" constitute the most active elements in modern Western thinking. It is legitimate to recognize in the messianic structure of Marx's program for history and in the stoic pessimism of Freud's account of the human condition commanding strains of theological inheritance and metaphor. Nietzsche's doctrines of Will and of "eternal return" are explicitly post-theological. They are attempts to map human experience immediately following on the eclipse of God. It is difficult to avoid the impression—"impression" may be too cautious a word—that Heidegger's teachings on Being, on fallenness and authenticity, on being-unto-death and freedom, on language as *logos* are a meta-theology that sets the hidden presentness of Being in the place of a supernatural divinity. The occult foursome in Heidegger's later writings —"the gods, mortal man, the heavens, and the earth"— is explicable, if at all, only in terms of a metaphoric modulation from traditional theology into a kind of "mystery of immanence." This modulation is charged, as is the sum of Heidegger's vocabulary and argumentative procedures, with a theological legacy.

To many this will seem a meager yield. To logicians and positivists it will afford conclusive evidence of Heidegger's "mysticism." Neither seems to me an adequate response.

Even if, or just because, they are so graphically unanswerable, the questions Heidegger poses about the nature and meaning of existence have a compelling centrality. By asking them over and over again, he has drawn into novel and radically challenging focus numerous areas of human behavior, social history, and the history of thought. Heidegger's endeavor, very likely frustrated, to create a new idiom, to free the language of largely unexamined and often illusory metaphysical or "scientific" presuppositions is of great moment and fascination. His diagnosis of man's estrangement and servitude in a wasted ecology was prophetic, and it remains unsurpassed in seriousness and consequence. Even where one dissents from it, the Heideggerian re-evaluation of the development and ambiguous meaning of Western metaphysics from Plato to Nietzsche is profoundly stimulating. It literally forces one to attempt to rethink the very concept of thought. Only a major thinker can provoke so creatively. And in a way which Wittgenstein alone can match for dramatic (dare one say histrionic?) integrity, Heidegger has been the modern exemplar of a life given to the cause of intellectual, moral inquiry. Because Heidegger has been among us, the notion that the asking of questions is the supreme piety of the spirit, and the uncanny idea that abstract thought is man's preeminent excellence and burden have been affirmed.

Much in this massive, so frequently enigmatic and even unacceptable performance, remains uncertain. Philosophies and antiphilosophies to come will feed on it, most richly, perhaps, where they reject it. But Heidegger's fundamental question will stand, and it is Coleridge, in an almost literal anticipation, who summarizes it most acutely:

> Hast thou ever raised thy mind to the consideration of EXISTENCE, in and by itself, as the mere act of existing? Hast thou ever said to thyself, thoughtfully, IT IS! heedless in that moment, whether it were a man before thee, or a flower, or a grain of sand? Without reference, in short, to this or that particular mode or form

of existence? If thou hast indeed attained to this, thou wilt have felt the presence of a mystery, which must have fixed thy spirit in awe and wonder. The very words, There is nothing! or, There was a time, when there was nothing! are self-contradictory. There is that within us which repels the proposition with as full and instantaneous a light, as if it bore evidence against the fact in the right of its own eternity. [*The Friend* II, xi]

Martin Heidegger is the great master of astonishment, the man whose amazement before the blank fact that we *are* instead of *not being*, has put a radiant obstacle in the path of the obvious. His is the thought which makes even momentary condescension toward the fact of existence unforgivable. In the forest clearing to which his circular paths lead, though they do not reach it, Heidegger has postulated the unity of thought and of poetry, of thought, of poetry, and of that highest act of mortal pride and celebration which is to give thanks. There are meaner metaphors to live by.

BIOGRAPHICAL NOTE

1889	September 26, born in Messkirch.
1903–09	Schooling in the *Gymnasium*, first in Constance, then in Freiburg in Breisgau.
1909–13	Theological and philosophical studies at the University of Freiburg.
1916	Obtains his *Habilitation* (the qualification required for teaching at the university level) with a monograph on Duns Scotus.
1917	Marriage to Elfriede Petri.
1922	Appointed to teach philosophy at the University of Marburg.
1927	Publication of *Sein und Zeit*.
1928	Succeeds his master and teacher Edmund Husserl in the chair of philosophy at Freiburg.
1929	At colloquium at Davos debates against Ernst Cassirer.
1933	April, chosen to be rector of the University.
1934	February, resigns his rectorship.
1944	Enrolled in a work brigade.
1945–51	Under the de-Nazification rules laid down by the Allied authorities, placed under *Lehrverbot* (a prohibition to teach in any public capacity).
1951	Resumes his professorship with a seminar on Aristotle's *Physics*. Appointed honorary professor, and continues to give occasional seminars until 1967.
1955	First visit to France, returning in 1966, 1968, and 1969 to give seminars at Thor, Provence, to a group of French admirers and disciples, which includes the painter Georges Braque and the poet René Char.
1962	First visit to Greece.
1976	May 26, death, in Messkirch. Buried in the graveyard which he passed daily as a schoolboy. Publication of the first two volumes of the planned *Gesamtausgabe* ("Complete Works").

SHORT BIBLIOGRAPHY

WORKS BY HEIDEGGER AVAILABLE IN ENGLISH

Individual Volumes

What Is Philosophy?, tr. W. Kluback and J. T. Wilde (New York: Twayne Publishers, Inc., 1958).

The Question of Being, tr. W. Kluback and J. T. Wilde (New York: Twayne Publishers, Inc., 1959).

Introduction to Metaphysics, tr. Ralph Manheim (New Haven: Yale University Press, 1959).

Being and Time, tr. John Macquarrie and Edward Robinson (New York: Harper & Row, 1962).

Kant and the Problem of Metaphysics, tr. James S. Churchill (Bloomington: Indiana University Press, 1962).

What Is a Thing?, tr. W. B. Barton, Jr., and Vera Deutsch (Chicago: Henry Regnery Co., 1968).

What Is Called Thinking?, tr. F. D. Wieck and J. G. Gray (New York: Harper & Row, 1968).

Discourse on Thinking, tr. J. M. Anderson and E. H. Freund (New York: Harper & Row, 1969).

Identity and Difference, tr. J. Stambaugh (New York: Harper & Row, 1969).

Poetry, Language, Thought, tr. Albert Hofstadter (New York: Harper & Row, 1972).

The End of Philosophy, tr. J. Stambaugh (New York: Harper & Row, 1973).

Collections

Existence and Being—tr. Douglas Scott: "Remembrance of the Poet," "Hölderlin and the Essence of Poetry"; tr. R. F. C. Hull and Alan Crick: "On the Essence of Truth," "What Is Metaphysics?"—ed. Werner Broch (Chicago: Henry Regnery Co., 1950).

Poetry, Language, Thought—"The Thinker as Poet," "The Origin of the Work of Art," "What Are Poets For?" "Building Dwelling Thinking," "The Thing," "Language," ". . . Poetically Man Dwells . . ."—tr. Albert Hofstadter (New York: Harper & Row, 1972).

On the Way to Language—tr. Peter D. Hertz: "Language in the Poem," "A Dialogue on Language," "The Essence of Language," "The Way to Language"; tr. Joan Stambaugh: "Words" (New York: Harper & Row, 1971).

The End of Philosophy—"Metaphysics as History of Being," "Sketches for a History of Being as Metaphysics," "Recollection in Metaphysics," "Overcoming Metaphysics"—tr. Joan Stambaugh (New York: Harper & Row, 1973).

Early Greek Thinking—"The Anaximander Fragment," "Logos (Heraclitus, Fragment B50)," "Moira (Parmenides, VIII, 34–41)," "Aletheia (Heraclitus, Fragment B16)"—tr. David F. Krell and Frank A. Capuzzi (New York: Harper & Row, 1975).

The Piety of Thinking—"Phenomenology and Theology," "The Problem of a Non-Objectifying Thinking and Speaking in Today's Theology," "Review of Ernst Cassirer's *Mythical Thinking*," "Principles of Thinking"—tr. James G. Hart and John C. Maraldo (Bloomington: Indiana University Press, 1976).

The Question Concerning Technology: Heidegger's Critique of the Modern Age—"The Question Concerning Technology," "The Turning," "The Word of Nietzsche: 'God is Dead,' " "The Age of the World Picture," "Science and Reflection" —tr. William Lovitt (New York: Harper & Row, 1977).

Basic Writings—tr. Joan Stambaugh: "Introduction to *Being and Time*," "The End of Philosophy and the Task of Thinking"; tr. David F. Krell: "What Is Metaphysics?"; tr. J. Glenn Gray: "On the Essence of Truth" (with Fred D. Wieck), "What Calls for Thinking?"; tr. Albert Hofstadter: "The Origin of the Work of Art," "Building Dwelling Thinking"; tr. W. B. Barton, Jr., and Vera Deutsch: "Modern Science, Metaphysics, and Mathematics"; tr. William Lovitt: "The Question Concerning Technology"—ed. David F. Krell (New York: Harper & Row, 1977).

Nietzsche IV: Nihilism—"European Nihilism," "Nihilism and the History of Being"—tr. Frank A. Capuzzi, ed. David F. Krell (New York, 1978).

Nietzsche I: Will to Power as Art—"Will to Power as Art"— tr. David F. Krell (New York, forthcoming).

Nietzsche II: The Eternal Recurrence of the Same—"The Eternal Recurrence of the Same," "Who Is Nietzsche's Zarathustra?"—tr. David F. Krell (New York, forthcoming).

Nietzsche III: Will to Power as Knowledge and as Metaphysics
—"The Will to Power as Knowledge," "The Eternal Recurrence of the Same and the Will to Power," "Nietzsche's Metaphysics"—tr. David F. Krell (New York, forthcoming).

In Anthologies and Journals

Introduction to *What Is Metaphysics?*, tr. Walter Kaufman, in *Existentialism from Dostoevsky to Sartre* (New York: Meridian Books, Inc., 1956).
"Letter on Humanism," tr. Edgar Lohner, in *Philosophy in the Twentieth Century* 3, ed. William Barrett and Henry D. Aiken (New York, 1962).
"The Age of the World View," tr. Marjorie Grene, in *Boundary* 24 (1976).

FURTHER READING

The bibliography of books and articles on Heidegger now contains more than four thousand items. The greater part of the literature can be found listed in Hans-Martin Sass: *Heidegger-Bibliographie* (Meisenheim am Glan, 1968) and *Materialien zu Heidegger-Bibliographie 1917–71* (Meisenheim, 1975).

The best short introduction is Winfried Franzen's *Martin Heidegger* (Stuttgart, 1976), which itself contains important bibliographies. The English-speaking reader will find the following of especial help:

Wyschogrod, M., *Kierkeggard and Heidegger* (London, 1954).
Richardson, William J., *Heidegger: Through Phenomenology to Thought* (The Hague, 1963).
Seidel, George J., *Martin Heidegger and the Pre-Socratics* (University of Nebraska Press, 1964).
Gelven, Michael, *A Commentary on Heidegger's "Being and Time"* (New York: Harper & Row, 1970).
Biemel, Walter, *Martin Heidegger* (London: Routledge & Paul, 1977), a collection of documents and pictures.
Murray, Michael, ed., *Heidegger and Modern Philosophy: Critical Essays* (New Haven: Yale University Press, 1978), which contains a complete bibliography of Heidegger's appearances in English.

Anyone wishing to make up his mind about Heidegger's political involvement will want to look at the following:

Weill, Eric, "Le Cas Heidegger," in *Les Temps modernes* III (Paris, 1947).

Löwith, K., *Heidegger, Denker in dürftiger Zeit* (Hamburg, 1953).

Uhnerfeld, Paul, *In Sachen Heidegger* (Hamburg, 1959, 1961).

Schneeberger, Guido, *Nachlese zu Heidegger* (Bern, 1962).

Adorno, T. W., *Jargon der Eigentlichkeit* (Frankfurt a. M., 1964).

Schwan, A., *Politische Philosophie im Denken Heideggers* (1965).

Fédier, F., "Trois attaques contre Heidegger, in *Critique* 234 (Paris, 1966).

——, "A Propos de Heidegger: une lecture dénoncée," in *Critique* 242 (1967).

——, "A Propos de Heidegger," in *Critique* 251 (1967). Ripostes and counterstatements by R. Minder and J. P. Faye appeared in *Critique* 237 (1967).

Alleman, Beda, "Heidegger und die Poitik," in *Merkur* XXI (Munich, 1967).

Palmier, Jean-Michel, *Les Escrits politiques de Heidegger* (Paris, 1968), a compilation to be used with extreme caution.

Interview with Heidegger, published posthumously in *Der Spiegel* XXIII (1976).

Pachter, H., "Heidegger and Hitler," in *Boston University Journal* XXIV (1976).

Barrett, William, "Homeless in the World," in *Commentary* (New York, 1976), an attempt at a conciliatory view, the more striking for having appeared in the organ of American Jewish liberal thought.

Bronner, S., "Heidegger's Politics," in *Salmagundi* (Saratoga Springs, N.Y., 1977).

Other works on Heidegger, mentioned in the text and not yet listed here, are:

Weizacker, C. F. von, "Allgemeinheit und Gewissenheit," in G. Neske, ed., *Martin Heidegger zum Siebzigsten Geburtstag* (Pfullingen, 1959).

Apel, K. O., "Wittgenstein und Heidegger. Die Frage nach dem Sinn und das Problem der 'Geisteswissenschaften,' " in *Philosophisches Jahrbuch* 72 (Freiburg, 1965).

Lévinas, Emmanuel, *En Découvrant l'existence avec Husserl et Heidegger* (Paris, 1967).

Minder, R., "Heidegger und Hebel oder die Sprache von Messkirche," in *Hölderlin unter den Deutschen* (Frankfurt, 1968).

Apel, K. O., "Wittgenstein und Heidegger. Die Frage nach dem Sinn von Sein und der Sinnlosigkeits verdacht gegen alle Metaphysik," in O. Pöggeler, ed., *Heidegger: Perspektiven zur Deutung Seines Werks* (Cologne, 1969).

Maurer, Reinhart, "Der Angewandte Heidegger," in *Philosophisches Jahrbuch* 77 (Freiburg, 1970).

Gadamer, Hans-Georg, *Truth and Method* (New York, 1975).

Böschenstein, Bernhard, "Die Dichtung Hölderlins," in *Zeitwende* 48 (Lahr, 1977).

Goldmann, Lucien, *Lukács et Heidegger* (Paris, 1977).

INDEX

Aders, Charles, 111
Adorno, Theodor W., 9, 12, 111*n.*
Agrarianism, 148–49
Aichinger, Ilse, 152
Aletheia (truth), 68, 114, 115
Alienation, crisis of, 39, 93, 109, 147, 154
Alltäglichkeit, 82
Anaximander, 5, 27, 150
Angst, 74, 79, 94, 96, 100, 105, 106, 108, 133
Annunciation (Fra Angelico), 130
Anomie, Durkheim's concept of, 93, 147
Antigone (Sophocles), 51, 103, 141, 142, 144, 145
Apel, K. O., 150–51
Aquinas, Thomas, 2, 4
Arendt, Hannah, 6, 116
Aristotelian logic, 1, 14
Aristotelian substance, 23, 28, 48, 65, 80
Aristotle, 4, 5, 23, 28, 34, 38, 55, 60, 62, 63, 64, 69, 81, 115, 129, 130, 150
Art, 132–36; as instauration, 135
Astonishment at being, 26, 27, 30, 31, 35, 54, 65, 158
Augustine, Saint, 74, 78, 79, 101, 102, 147
Aus der Geschichte des Seyns (Heidegger), 2
Austin, J. L., 14
Ayer, A. J., 154

Bach, Johann Sebastian, 125
Bachmann, Ingeborg, 152
Bacon, Francis, 55, 115
Barrès, Maurice, 149
Barth, Karl, 73
Bauen, 130, 131
Beaufret, Jean, 33
Beethoven, Ludwig van, 125

Being and Nothingness (*L'Etre et le néant*, Sartre), 10
Being and Time (*Sein und Zeit*, Heidegger), 2, 3, 5, 7, 8, 11, 13, 18, 28, 30, 33, 34, 47, 53, 60, 61, 62, 63, 74–81 *passim*, 87, 90, 96, 99, 101, 102, 106, 107, 111–17 *passim*, 127, 128, 129, 132, 133, 148; "anthropological" sections of, 86; and Nazism, 116, 119, 121, 122, 123; prepares *Dasein* for apprehension of Being, 153; as reprise of Kierkegaard, 147; Ryle's review of, 151; singularity of, 76–77; termination of, in midstream, 113; unity of being and time stressed in, 78; *see also Dasein;* Ontology, Heidegger's; *Sein*
Being in being, Heidegger's discussion of, 25–33, 37, 67, 81; *see also Dasein;* Ontology, Heidegger's; *Sein*
"Beingquestion" (*Seinsfrage*), 33–38, 40, 45, 53, 54, 64, 81, 82
Being-toward-death (*Seinzum-Tode*), 102, 104, 105
Benn, Gottfried, 149
Bergson, Henri, 65
Binswanger, L., 151
Blick ins Chaos (Hesse), 76
Bloch, Ernest, 104, 148
Bollack, H., 152
Bollnow, O. F., 76
Böschenstein, Bernhard, 143
Boss, M., 151
Braque, Georges, 17
Brentano, Franz, 16, 34, 64
Brief über den Humanismus: see *Letter on "Humanism"*
Buber, Martin, 124
Bultmann, Rudolf, 5, 73, 151